MANX CROSSES

A HANDBOOK OF STONE SCULPTURE
500-1040 IN THE ISLE OF MAN

MANX CROSSES

A HANDBOOK OF STONE SCULPTURE 500-1040 IN THE ISLE OF MAN

David M. Wilson

ARCHAEOPRESS ARCHAEOLOGY

ARCHAEOPRESS PUBLISHING LTD.

Gordon House
276 Banbury Road
Oxford OX2 7ED
www.archaeopress.com

ISBN 978-1-784917-56-2 (paperback)
978-1-784917-57-9 (hardback)

Published by Manx National Heritage
in association with Archaeopress

© Manx National Heritage 2018

Designed by Valerie Cottle

Printed and bound in England
by Shortrun Press Ltd., Devon

This book is available direct from Archaeopress
or from our website www.archaeopress.com

Contents

PREFACE

I MAKE NO EXCUSES for writing this book. The stone sculptures of the first five centuries of Christianity in the Isle of Man have not been discussed as a whole since the publication of P. M. C. Kermode's magnificent catalogue and discussion of the subject in 1907. I cannot emulate him, nor will I attempt to. I can, however, comment on the sculptures in some depth, particularly since the pre-Scandinavian-influenced crosses have received little published attention during the last century, while the crosses of the Scandinavian settlers of the Island have suffered from a massive amount of comment, but little synthesis.

This is a book for the general, but enquiring, reader. It is a work of synthesis, and not a catalogue, although a hand-list of all the 200-plus sculptures (more than double the number of those known to Kermode) is included as an appendix. This records provenances and, where possible, references to images of them all.

Academic and public interest in the 'Viking' world in the last fifty years has led to an explosion in literature, both learned and popular, with which it is impossible to keep up to date. Hidden amongst this academic literature are analyses in depth of details of the internationally important material remains of the period of Scandinavian settlement of the Isle of Man, together with a (very) few attempts at synthesis. In this book I have attempted a synthesis of the story of early Manx sculpture from the earliest period of Christianity in the sixth century to the early eleventh century – a story for which the sculpture provides the only coherent evidence of a continuous development.

The story told is set against the fragmentary recorded background of political, religious, economic and social circumstances of the Island, and of the connections of the Manx people to their neighbours and to the wider world outside.

★   ★   ★   ★   ★

A few technical explanations are necessary. As in most parts of the United Kingdom, spelling of place-names varies according to available sources at the time of standardisation by nineteenth-century surveyors, which themselves were not always correct. Spelling was often spelled phonetically by men unfamiliar with the Manx language, while antiquarians sometimes romanticised spellings, the most egregious example in the Isle of Man being 'Conchan' for 'Onchan'. I have, therefore, standardised all spellings according to George Broderick's *Placenames of the Isle of Man* (Tübingen, 1994-2005). The one exception is the almost universal spelling 'Santon', rather than the intermittently used parish name 'Santan', which Broderick seems to prefer. Hyphenation follows Broderick, e.g. 'Knock y Doonee', not 'Knock-y-Doonee'.

Although naturally preferring the Authorised Version, I have used the modern translation of the Bible, *The New English Bible*, as this translation is likely to be more accurate.

Rather than using footnotes, endnotes or other in-text references, I have provided a discursive bibliography of easily-obtainable sources to aid further study. I would particularly refer to the forthcoming catalogue by M. P. Barnes and J. Knirk, *The runic inscriptions of the Isle of Man* (Uppsala), which will appear shortly, which records and dissects the important series of Scandinavian runic texts on the stones.

Text photographs have presented a problem. There is no available standardised series of quality photographs of the monuments. As this book goes to press I have learned that a systematic high-technology series of images of the stones is planned; but, for reasons of cost and also because of the awkward placing of many stones, this is likely to take some time to produce. In any case, the ornament on many sculptures has been badly worn by exposure to the elements (this is particularly true of some of the Maughold series, which have been wilfully neglected for many years). I have tried, therefore, to gather the best possible pictures – some more than 100 years old – for the purposes of this book from a number of sources, particularly from the archive of Manx National Heritage, from which the majority of figures has been derived, and which are copyright of the Trustees.

The copyright of other photographs and drawings is gratefully acknowledged to the following: fig. 14, The Trustees of the British Museum; figs. 48, 53, The British Academy Corpus of Anglo-Saxon Stone Sculpture: fig. 46, ATA Stockholm; fig. 8, Ross Trench-Jellicoe; fig. 2 above, after G. Bersu and D. M. Wilson; figs. 32, 34, 36, 37, 45, Eva Wilson; figs. 3 right,

5, 26 right, 41 right, 52 left, 56, 58, 62, Joseph Payne; figs. 18, 22, 27, 39, 40, 44, 50, 54 and 57, Andrew Johnson; fig. 7, A. C. Thomas; figs. 2 below, 20, 26, 28, 41 left, 47, D. M. Wilson. Vic Bates has drawn the map (fig. 1), and Valerie Cottle provided the photograph for the front cover.

A large number of people have helped in the writing of this book. First, the staff of the Manx Museum; particularly Wendy Thirkettle and the staff of the library. Allison Fox and Andrew Johnson have been a constant support; Andrew particularly has saved me very many numerical errors in the main text and the appendix, caused by my congenital inability to transcribe figures accurately. The staff of the Library of the Society of Antiquaries of London have helped in many ways, particularly in providing photocopies during my frequent visits. Joseph Payne has taken numerous photographs, some of which are published and acknowledged here, and he must be thanked for his skill and patience. Barbara Doyle has driven me around. Wendy Davies and Colleen Batey have answered questions. Damian McManus has advised me on ogams. Dave Quirk has provided me with exhaustive information concerning the geology of the Island, and Derek Craig has fed me information on Galloway.

Especial thanks must go to Michael Barnes for help with runes. He also provided me with pre-publication transcriptions and transliterations of all the Manx Scandinavian runic inscriptions, some of which I have used here. Judith Jesch read my chapter on the runic inscriptions and corrected my errors. Most importantly, James Graham-Campbell and Else Roesdahl read the whole of the main text in draft and helped clear up obfuscations and throw out crazy ideas. They have done this over many years and my gratitude to them is unbounded. Valerie Cottle read and copy-edited my text, her eagle eye spotting and correcting typos and grammatical errors. She also designed the layout of the whole book with patience and skill; without her help it would not have appeared. Neither would it have appeared if the Director and Trustees of Manx National Heritage had not encouraged me to write it.

Lastly, I must thank Eva for keeping her temper throughout this long struggle. She it was who drove me round the Island in the years after my retirement, as I gathered information. In the course of the last three years she has also read drafts of the book, and fed and watered me with amazing fortitude and patience. It has been a good marriage!

David M. Wilson
Castletown, July 2017

THE CROSSES mentioned in this book are referred to by their Manx National Heritage registration numbers; these are indicated by having the number either painted on the cross, or on a metal disc. Most of those not illustrated here were originally pictured in accurate drawings or photographs published in P. M. C. Kermode's Manx Crosses, *1907. The work was re-published in a second edition, Balgavies, 1994. This edition, which is still in print and easily available, contains reprints of Kermode's later articles up to 1929. References to pictures in Kermode's work after 1929 will be found in the tables of the Appendix here (pages 151-71).*

CHAPTER 1
An introduction to the Island

THE ISLE OF MAN is rich in monuments of its past, but the most important, both nationally and internationally, are the remarkable series of decorated carved stone memorials and simpler grave-markers which span the early years of Christianity in the Island from the early sixth century to the first quarter of the eleventh century. The stones have been much studied and commented on since the early years of the eighteenth century by scholars in English and Scandinavian universities. Just over 200 complete or fragmentary memorials have been registered by Manx National Heritage, about fifty of which are simple, sharply-cut linear crosses, which are undatable but come from excavations at early burial grounds. The rest are worthy of examination, and many are full of information.

Most of the monuments are carved from the local mudstone. Often conveniently described as slate, technically they comprise various laminated mudstones, sometimes with sandstone interfaces, and come from various specific areas of the Island. A small number are of local granite, others are of various other local stones. Although no quarries of the early Christian period have been recognised, stone-carvers could easily have removed slabs from the exposed rock faces which form much of the rocky coastline or are exposed in the mountainous spine of the Island, a spine which rises to a height of 621m. Occasionally, glacial erratics or stone from major exposed outcrops of limestone bedrock in the south of the Island or sandstone in the west were used by the sculptors.

Physical geography

The Island at the beginning of the Holocene, some 12,000 years ago, had finally lost any overlying ice; man had moved in and had begun to make his own impression on the landscape. While geology has given a physical base to the Island, wild seas and glaciations have modified its form, providing it with shape and protecting it with rugged cliffs. Sheltered inlets and beaches, upland pastures and, in parts, fertile soil in the lowlands, provided a

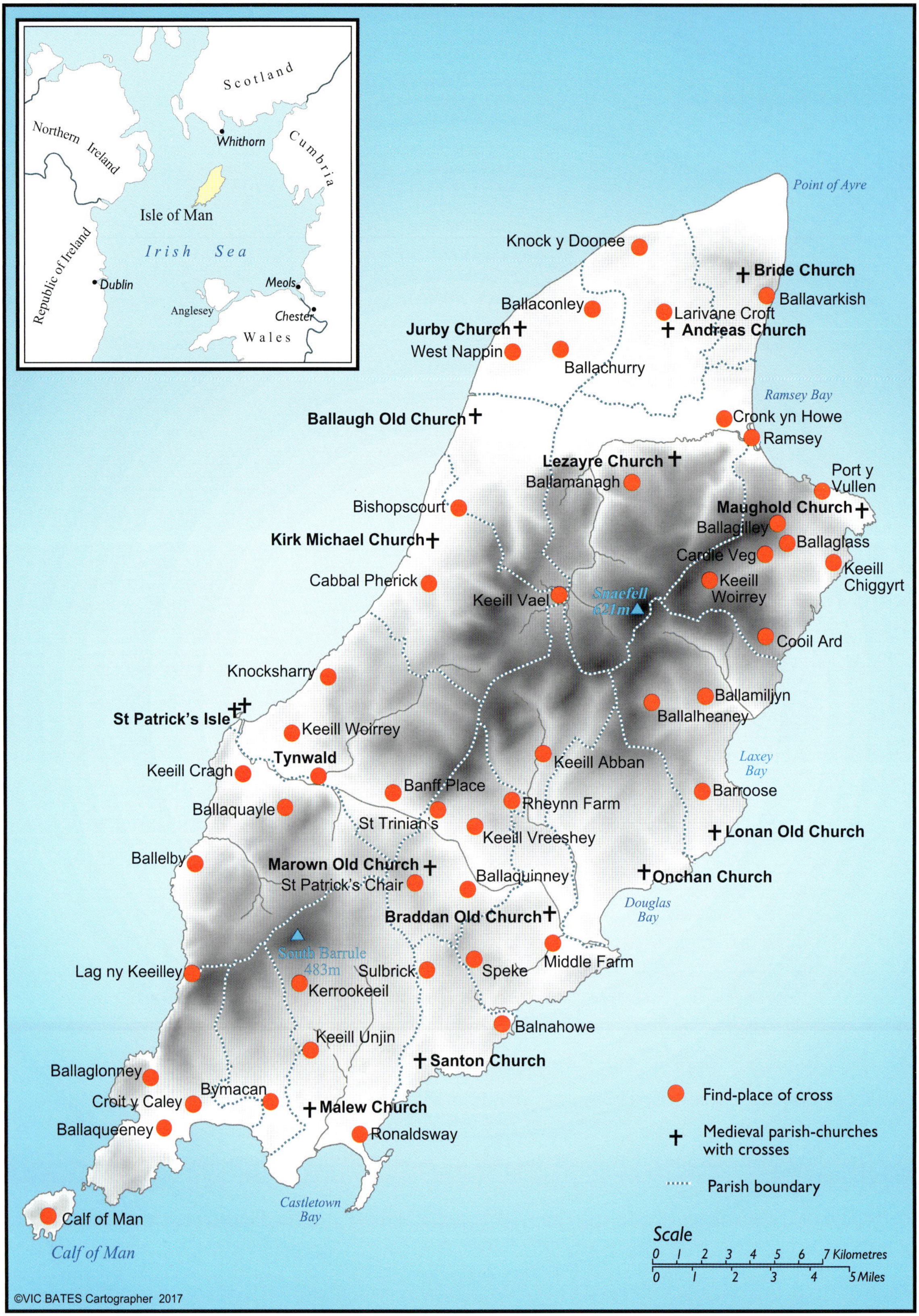

Inset map labels

Scotland

Whithorn

Cumbria

Northern Ireland

Isle of Man

Republic of Ireland

Irish Sea

Dublin

Meols

Anglesey

Chester

Wales

Main map labels

Point of Ayre

Knock y Doonee

+ **Bride Church**

Ballavarkish

Ballaconley

Larivane Croft

+ **Andreas Church**

Jurby Church +

West Nappin

Ballachurry

Ramsey Bay

Ballaugh Old Church +

Cronk yn Howe

Ramsey

Lezayre Church +

Ballamanagh

Port y Vullen

Maughold Church +

Bishopscourt

Ballagilley

Ballaglass

Kirk Michael Church +

Cardle Veg

Keeill Chiggyrt

Cabbal Pherick

Keeill Woirrey

Keeill Vael

Snaefell △621m

Cooil Ard

Knocksharry

Ballamillyn

Ballalheaney

St Patrick's Isle ++

Keeill Woirrey

Laxey Bay

Tynwald

Keeill Abban

Keeill Cragh

Banff Place

Barroose

Ballaquayle

Rheynn Farm

St Trinian's

+ **Lonan Old Church**

Keeill Vreeshey

Ballelby

Marown Old Church +

St Patrick's Chair

Ballaquinney

+ **Onchan Church**

Braddan Old Church +

Douglas Bay

△ South Barrule 483m

Lag ny Keeilley

Sulbrick

Speke

Middle Farm

Kerrookeeil

Keeill Unjin

Balnahowe

Ballaglonney

+ **Santon Church**

Bymacan

Croit y Caley

+ **Malew Church**

Ballaqueeney

Ronaldsway

Castletown Bay

● Calf of Man

Calf of Man

Legend

● Find-place of cross

+ Medieval parish-churches with crosses

...... Parish boundary

Scale

```
0   1   2   3   4   5   6   7 Kilometres
0       1       2       3       4   5 Miles
```

©VIC BATES Cartographer 2017

mixed farming economy which could be supplemented by fishing and rich mineral resources.

The Island's geography is important in the context of this book. It sits in the north-west corner of the Irish Sea, easily visible from the surrounding countries – England, Ireland, Scotland and Wales. From the Isle of Whithorn in Galloway off the southern tip of Scotland – the nearest land and an important point of contact in the early Christian period – the Island appears as a pyramidal outcrop, like a single mountain, and takes various guises when seen from the other three countries. In plan (fig. 1) it appears as a slightly lopsided lozenge, running NNE/SSW. Its greatest length is 45km, and at its widest it measures 16km; to the south is a small islet – the Calf of Man, now uninhabited. The main island is surrounded by a complex tidal system with a 7m fall; fierce currents and strong winds would not have encouraged strangers to land save in the calmest conditions, and then only in inlets protected from the weather, or on sandy beaches (preferably both). Such landing places sometimes retain in their names their interest to the Scandinavian settlers, terminating in the element -wick (from Old Norse –*vik*; 'bay' or 'inlet') as, for example, Fleshwick and Garwick.

No coherent written history of the Island is known before the mid-eleventh century; knowledge of its inhabitants and of its political and ecclesiastical structure before this date depends on occasional epigraphic material, casual mentions in Latin, English, Welsh and Irish written sources, and evidence provided almost incidentally by archaeology. The Romans must have visited the Isle of Man – they could see it from the Cumbrian coast, which they controlled – but have left no reliable physical traces on the Island apart from a handful of coins and a few Romano-British brooches. There is a possibility that it is the island *Monapia* mentioned in the first century AD by Pliny the Younger, and, in the second century, by the Greek geographer, Ptolemy. The identification in early sources is complicated by the fact that the names of Man and of Anglesey (modern Welsh *Môn*) were possibly confused at this period. The first indication that there

---

Fig. 1 (left). Plotted are the find-spots of the monuments discussed in this book. Omitted are a few sites of doubtful identity. The medieval parish boundaries are indicated. Churches symbolised on the map represent parish churchyards which, having produced crosses, were presumably burial grounds before the organisation of parishes in the thirteenth century. The two parish churches in the south-west, Rushen and Arbory, are unmarked, as their churchyards have produced no crosses.

were two islands with similar (or even identical) names appears in an early eighth-century English source, Bede's *Ecclesiastical History of the English People*, where he refers to two Mevanian islands, 'which are situated between Ireland and Britain…' being brought under the control of the North-umbrian king Edwin, although some historians have postulated that this control was in effect simply a spiritual authority. The first incontrovertible mention of the Island on its home ground is a runic inscription on one of the monuments which are the subject of this book, a cross-slab set up towards the middle of the tenth century by a Norse settler, and inscribed by a Scandinavian called Gautr, which refers to the fact that he carved that cross 'and all in Man (**maun**)' (p.130f and fig. 32).

The Island was not poor. First, it is rich in minerals – particularly lead and copper – which have allegedly been mined since the Bronze Age, while from the end of the Long Iron Age it had a small craft community making objects out of these metals. Later, from the ninth century onwards, there is growing evidence from metal-detector finds of a burgeoning metalwork production, which may have fed a small export industry from a number of beach markets. Mainly, however, its natural economy at this period rested on agriculture. The land would have been productive in the early Christian period, although of this we have practically no physical evidence. The uplands are generally of inhospitable heathland, useful mainly for grazing sheep, as they have been since the Bronze Age. By the beginning of the first millennium it is assumed that the varied woodland cover of the prehistoric period had been seriously depleted, save in the glens and gullies. The northern plain, with its moraine-derived deposits of sands and gravels, would have provided light soils suitable for the primitive ploughs of the time. The heavier soil of the south included a smallish area of rich soil based on the limestone, backed by a considerable productive area fror the growing of grain. The coastal land above the cliff-tops also provided for mixed faming. The main rivers held fish, including salmon, whilst shellfish and marine species, including seal, could have added to the diet – but of this there is little evidence. All these resources would have provided a reasonable living for the native population. Bede, at the beginning of the eighth century, records that it comprised more than 300 *familia* – i.e. major farmers and their households; other land would be reserved for royal, military or religious establishments. Bede compares it with Anglesey, which had three times the number of *familia* – but it should be pointed out that the Isle of Man has much more moorland, suitable only for rough grazing.

The kingdoms of the Irish Sea in the fifth to eighth centuries

From the Island on a clear day all the surrounding countries of the Irish Sea – known since the Middle Ages as Scotland, England, Wales and Ireland – can be seen. After the collapse of Roman power in Britain in the early years of the fifth century, it is assumed that the British tribes in the north and west of Britain gradually formed a series of kingdoms, often poorly recorded and difficult to define, which gradually formed recognisable polities. Knowledge of the social and political structure and control of the Island at this time is practically non-existent, but from archaeology it is clear that there was a continuity of native settlement from the pre-Roman Iron Age onwards. In the course of the first millennium, however, the Island became increasingly at risk from seaborne attack, first from Northumbria and then from Ireland, until in the late ninth century it became susceptible to attacks by raiders from Norway and from members of a Scandinavian diaspora in Shetland, Orkney, the Western Isles of Scotland and the Irish Sea region. Detail of the political structure in the encircling land mass from the fifth to the eighth century is complicated, as power structures were changed by powerful leaders using military force; their story can only be teased out by specialists from disparate written sources, often of doubtful quality, to help reconstruct the outside influences which brought Christianity and its visible symbols to the Island.

To the west was Ireland, a land made up of a number of major and minor kingdoms which defy simple mapping, of which Dál Riata was at its most important and influential in the sixth and seventh century. This kingdom was unique in that it not only had its major power base in County Antrim in the north-east of what is now Ulster, but also spanned the northern tip of the North Channel to control the southern Hebrides and parts of the mainland as far as the shadowy British kingdom of Strathclyde. To the east it bordered on the lands of the southern Picts, whose kings, having displaced the native British rulers centred on Dumbarton, gradually gained control of much of the north and east of Scotland north of the Forth (the Picts' boundary with the northern Anglo-Saxon kingdom of Northumbria). Northumbria was originally made up of two kingdoms: Bernicia to the north and Deira (basically Yorkshire and also ultimately Lancashire and Cumbria). To the south of Dál Riata, Galloway and the north shore of the Solway formed the core of the British kingdom of Rheged, the size of which is much discussed, but which in the early seventh century (probably not later than *c.*638) became part of the growing Anglian kingdom of Northumbria, possibly with one centre of power in Carlisle. Cumbria itself had only gradually become part of Northumbria, probably ruled by British chieftains, and had almost certainly reverted to paganism. If the Church founded by the Romans had survived in this region at all, it had little influence and was ripe for conversion by a gradually-expanding Northumbria.

From the early years of the seventh century Northumbria, to some extent unified and converted, had grown both geographically and in secular power, abutting the kingdom of the Picts to the north, as well as taking control of Rheged and the modern counties of Dumfries, Galloway, Cumbria and Lancashire. For a short period in the early seventh century, under the Northumbrian king Edwin, it possibly included the Isle of Man. However, by the end of the century, according to Irish sources, the Island was controlled by various British chieftains, who harried the coasts of Ulster and Leinster. To the south-west, Northumbria bordered the Mercian kingdom at the Mersey. Until the late tenth century (and in reality later) England south of Northumbria was also fragmented, but was gradually united in a union which included Northumbria.

To the south of the Isle of Man was the troubled kingdom of Gwynedd in North Wales. Since the Romans had retreated from Britain it had been constantly riven by problems of succession, division and expansive ambition. Harried by English, Irish and Scandinavian raids or invasions, its history is complex; it was intermittently at the height of its power between the ninth and eleventh century under various, often quarrelling, kings, when in theory it stretched from Anglesey to the Dee estuary.

Christianity

The Christian Church first made itself felt in Britain in the third century, at a period when it was a remote part of an empire which was officially Christian. But the Roman Empire was soon to collapse and, as its power and influence waned, Christianity gradually, if fitfully, spread under influence from Gaul throughout the non-Romanised areas of western Britain as far as Ireland. But it did not reach Scotland, while some (but not all) of Anglo-Saxon England reverted to paganism. It is in the form of inscriptions on stones raised by early British Christians, probably in the late fifth, or early sixth, century that traces of this early Christianity are first found in the Isle of Man. These stones and their successors form the subject of this book. Consequently, it is important to appreciate in the briefest of outlines something of the complicated story of the early Christian Church in Britain and Ireland between the end of the Roman Empire in the early fifth century, and the consequences of the Augustinian mission of the late sixth century. Only thus is it possible to surmise the process of conversion in the Isle of Man.

The British Church, which is sometimes – persistently, if incorrectly – labelled the 'Celtic Church', grew out of the Romano-British Church to become firmly established in the west of the geographical area known as the British Isles; that is, in the linguistic group of regions consisting, in modern terms, of Ireland, Cornwall, Wales, Man, Cumbria and Scotland. In view of the questionable identity and political background of the inhabitants of these regions, the Church is perhaps best referred to as the 'Western Church', a clumsy phrase with little meaning which will be avoided as much as possible in this book. The first named man associated with the conversion of Ireland was Palladius, a bishop sent by Pope Celestine to Ireland in 431 to minister to 'the Irish believing in Christ', but his reputation has been overshadowed by Patrick, who was to become the patron saint of Ireland. Indeed, many of Palladius' achievements were later attributed to Patrick, to the extent that most of his recorded deeds were subsumed into the hagiography of St Patrick. The Irish Church had, in effect, grown gradually from the official Christian religion of the Roman Empire.

Tradition would have it that Patrick was a Romano-British citizen from northern England who was sent to Ireland to formalise the Church of those Christians already existing there, and to preach the faith. (A similar story is told of the shadowy figure of St Ninian, about whom much less is known, who brought Christianity to Galloway, where his activities were centred on Whithorn). Two documents, surviving in later manuscript sources, are supposedly written by Patrick (his *Confessio* and *Epistoli*), which provide some sort of outline of his life. It is generally agreed that Patrick was born in Britain *c.*420, was admitted to the priesthood in southern Gaul, and that his main period of activity in Ireland was in the middle of the fifth century. A tradition that the Isle of Man was converted by Patrick is founded, first, on very dubious evidence in one twelfth-century Irish source, the *Lebor Gabála Érenn*, which spins a most unlikely tale, including the killing of three pagan gods. The second source for the story of Manx conversion is a circumstantial twelfth-century life (the *Vita Patricii*) by the hagiographer Jocelin of Furness, who was almost certainly making propaganda for the wife of one of his own patrons. But the Patrician tradition was strong and survives in the Island as the patronal name of two parish churches, Kirk Patrick and Jurby. It also survives as the name of St Patrick's Isle, the site of the now-ruined cathedral of the diocese of Sodor (later Sodor and Man) – all first recorded in the fifteenth or sixteenth century.

The official Church in Ireland (if it can be so designated), or much of it, seems to have disapproved of Patrick, whose mission was unorthodox and to some extent venal. He had no territorial base in Ireland until the foundation of the monastery of Armagh, traditionally *c*.444. Yet the Church for which he was partly responsible was presumably close in practice to that of Gaul and of the rest of western Britain, but without its structure. By the end of the sixth century, however, the great monasteries of Ireland, among them Clonmacnoise, Durrow and Derry, were well-established, as was an important outlier in Dál Riata, on the island of Iona off the west coast of Mull (founded by St Columba *c*.563). The powerful abbots of the Irish semi-secular monasteries were in many ways more important than the bishops who tended the Church spiritually; they it was, through such missionary foundations as Iona and Lindisfarne, who were to evangelise in Northumbria. In Gwynedd, where Christianity had built on foundations left by the departing Romans, a similar monastic establishment was growing, for example, at Bangor-is-y-coed, near Wrexham. According to the Northumbrian monk Bede, writing in the early eighth century, it comprised a population of some 2,000 monks, 'all of whom were accustomed to live by the labour of their hands' a life based on an organised (secular/aristocratic) tradition.

The conversion of Northumbria began in 625, following a mission by Paulinus (who had accompanied St Augustine from Rome to Kent to begin the conversion of England in 597). But Paulinus' mission was short-lived, and the Church lapsed into semi-paganism with the wasting of Northumbria and the death of the king, Edwin, at the hands of the pagan king, Penda of Mercia, and Cadwallon, king of Gwynedd, in 633. In the following year Cadwallon was killed in flight from Edwin's son, the victorious Oswald, at the battle of Hallington, and Oswald became king of Northumbria. Oswald in exile had taken refuge in Iona, 'the chief of nearly all the monasteries of the northern Irish and of all the monasteries of the Picts', during Edwin's reign, and had been baptised there. It was thus natural that he should in 635 choose a monk of that monastery, Aidan, to lead a mission to refresh the conversion of Northumbria. Aidan established a monastery on Lindisfarne, an island off the coast of Northumberland, which was to become the most important centre of Irish influence in this part of the kingdom.

From Lindisfarne were founded a number of major religious houses, and missionaries from Northumbria converted the rulers of the East Saxons, Middle Anglians and Mercians. In the course of the seventh century, with the growing authority of Rome, the Irish-influenced Northumbrian Church was in trouble. In 664 a synod of the Northumbrian king and members of the English and Irish hierarchies was held at a place called *Streanæshalch* (possibly Whitby), at which the Roman liturgy was introduced and, famously, the date of Easter was changed from the British to the Roman calendar. This meeting marked the beginning of great turbulence in the Church, a turbulence which involved both England and Ireland. One of the most influential figures present at the synod was Wilfrid, who, educated at Lindisfarne, had spent at least ten years in Rome. As one of the spokesmen for the Roman side at Whitby, he was almost immediately nominated by the king as Archbishop of York. Theodore of Tarsus (a Syrian), a man of formidable administrative ability and a great reformer in the tradition of Rome, was consecrated Archbishop of Canterbury in 668, and was to hold the see for twenty-two years. He restructured the English hierarchy and, confirming Wilfrid's appointment to York, indirectly but clearly reduced the Irish influence in Northumbria. Many of the Irish leaders now drifted back to Ireland by way of Iona. A leader of this group of exiled priests, a former bishop of Lindisfarne named Colmán, founded a monastery at Mayo for English priests who refused to accept the Roman rule imposed by the Synod of Whitby.

Wilfrid grew in importance, pursuing the Roman traditions of Whitby, and soon established regular Roman monasteries at Hexham and Ripon, which he held until after many adventures he was driven out of his diocese of York in 678 by King Ecgfrith. After appeals to Rome and special pleading with the great and good of his day, living on his various estates or at the monasteries he had founded, he ultimately ended up, with diminished authority as bishop in Ripon, where he died, aged seventy-five, in 709 or 710. One of his contemporaries was Benedict Biscop, who became the influential leader of the Roman party. Benedict was founder and first abbot and bishop of the rich double monastery of Monkwearmouth and Jarrow (in 674, and 680/1). With the aid of substantial land-grants from the king these twin monasteries flourished, and it was here that the great historian of the early English Church, the Venerable Bede, lived and worked from 679 until his death in 735.

The monastery of Whithorn in Galloway, traditionally founded by the British St Ninian who is said to have been consecrated in Rome in the late fifth or sixth century, hovered uneasily between Northumbria to the east, Ireland to the west and Pictland to the north. According to Bede, Whithorn had remained important enough, due to the recent increase in members of the Church, to be re-founded in 681 as one of four Northumbrian bishoprics. But it gradually declined and lost its episcopal status. The Northumbrian and Irish Churches, however, remained in friendly communication throughout what remained of the eighth century and beyond, their members constantly visiting each other or becoming temporary or permanent members of each others' community, travelling on vessels either owned or controlled by greater monasteries like Iona.

Geographically in the midst of all this ecclesiastical turmoil and development sat the Isle of Man, with a Church influenced from all sides of the Irish Sea. Here the Manx memorial stones begin to tell a tale of these influences, from both west and east. One place in the Island – the monastic community of Maughold, which is discussed in chapter 3 – was caught up in the middle of the vibrant cross-cultural Christian traffic between Northumbria, Scotland, Wales and Ireland, and its sculpture provides vital clues to this position.

This pared-down summary of the complicated origins of Christianity in the north and west of Britain has been necessary, as it provides a background to the tenuous picture of the origins and character of Manx Christianity which can be gleaned from written sources. Without the stone sculpture which is the subject of this book, we would know little or nothing about Manx Christianity in the first millennium AD. Without the sculpture, it might have been possible to suggest, but not demonstrate, that Christianity appeared, as it did in Ireland, as an unofficial religion in the dying years of the Roman Empire in the West. Alternatively, without the stones we might have hazarded a guess that the Isle of Man was converted by Palladius, Patrick or Ninian. Yet another possibility would have been to consider its introduction to the Island by later Irish intervention, or during the short period after the Northumbrian king, Edwin, had been converted by Paulinus and baptised at York in 627, only to be killed at Hatfield in 632. Elements of these theories – and others – remain possibilities, but the hard evidence provided by a close study of the sculptured stones enables us to establish a more coherent story.

CHAPTER 2

Early stones and sacred sites

THE EARLY HISTORY of Christianity in Britain clearly affects the Manx story told in this book. The new religion, as has been shown, first came to Britain in the late Roman period, but it was not until the late fifth century that it made its presence more strongly felt in western Britain generally. There is no evidence that Roman Christianity (or indeed any religion of the Roman Empire) affected the native population of the Island, but such a possibility cannot be totally dismissed. It may, however, reasonably be assumed that until the fifth century the Manx practised a pagan religion, perhaps similar to that encountered in England by Paulinus when in the early seventh century, as recounted by Bede in dramatic terms, he began the process of conversion in Northumbria. Paganism in the Isle of Man can only be detected in the ritual observed in the burial of the dead; but, although some graves survive, they tell little of the nature of the religion of the indigenous inhabitants. Until the arrival of Scandinavian settlers at the end of the ninth century, their graves have only been dated (in very few instances) by the radiocarbon method.

Generally, throughout the whole of the first millennium the dead of the Isle of Man were buried in small graveyards established on sites of familial or community remembrance and convenience, some of which continued in use without a break into the Scandinavian period and beyond. Only occasionally, as in the large cemetery on St Patrick's Isle, off the west coast, do cemeteries show this continuity. Although only a handful of burial sites have been recorded by excavation, at least 180 presumed small burial-grounds have been recognised and recorded in the course of the Manx Archaeological Survey's work on the *keeill* sites (for keeills see below, p.17f). Records show that burials occurred in some of these small cemeteries throughout the Middle Ages, even as late as the nineteenth century.

Bodies in the Christian period were generally buried in an extended position with heads to the west, often laid in cist graves (in the Island known as lintel graves), which are lined (fig. 2) and covered with slabs of mud-

Fig. 2 above. Lintel graves disturbed by a tenth-century boat-grave at Balladoole, Arbory, one of the few examples of such graves which are datable.

Below. Few recent burials have occurred in the old churchyard at Lonan, hence the plain slabs which presumably cover graves of lintel construction, but of relatively modern date.

stone quarried locally (fig. 2). This rite and practice followed a similar form, as in Scotland, Ireland and Northumbria, from the pre-Christian period into modern times. In the Isle of Man in the immediate period of Scandinavian settlement a few graves were furnished in the settlers' pagan fashion, with weapons or other objects (see chapter 4). It is clear that the graves would have been marked in some way, and that the markers after conversion to Christianity were sometimes more extravagant than the simple incised crosses on small wedge-shaped stones found on the few excavated sites. From the sixth to the early eleventh century memorial stones – some more elaborate than others – were erected in graveyards. Few stones have been found in direct relation to individual graves (a rare exception was a lintel grave with a simple ringed-cross as a marker – no. 204 – excavated by Andrew Johnson at Banff Place, Greeba, in 1995). It must be assumed, however, on the basis of epigraphical evidence that the memorial stones were initially provided for individuals and not for a group of people, unless a single stone commemorated the head of a family.

Inscriptions in Roman and ogam script on one pillar-like memorial, probably of seventh-century date, about 270 metres from a burial site at Knock y Doonee (Andreas 5; fig. 3 right), imply a relationship to dispersed burials around a keeill in the next field; other short inscriptions in a variety of scripts could have been erected to a similar mind-set. In at least one case in the eighth century an incised and inscribed stone was placed at the head and foot of a grave at Maughold (42 and 43; below p.35). Few distinctive pre-Scandinavian memorial slabs of this period are personalised, but one grand granite slab, Maughold 69 (figs. 9 and 10, p.27), has a discreet uncial inscription, placed uniquely at the top of one edge, recording that it is the cross of Guriat (see below p.26). On crosses of the Scandinavian period personalised runic inscriptions, often of some length, are frequently (but not universally) found. Down the centuries some stones, particularly those in churchyards in continuous use, collapsed and were discarded, and, their meaning having been lost, were sometimes re-used for walling or as lintels in both secular and religious buildings. Very occasionally they were re-used as tombstones in modern times (Kirk Michael 110 and Andreas 168).

While it is true that many stones were found in the churchyards of the medieval parish churches, elaborately decorated or inscribed stones have also been found on a fair number of burial sites, dating from the sixth century onwards, as, for example, the pillar found at Ballaqueeney, (fig. 3 left) in the south of the Island, or the elaborately decorated tenth-century cross

Fig. 3. Early sixth-century memorial pillars found on early burial-grounds. Left, from Ballaqueeney (Rushen 2: height 52cm). Right, from Knock y Doonee (Andreas 5: height 172cm). The latter stone was found near a tenth-century boat-burial, demonstrating the continuous use of the burial-ground from the sixth century onwards.

re-used as a lintel in the later but long-deserted chapel of Keeill Pheric at West Nappin (Jurby 103), in the north. The preponderance of parish churchyard finds is presumably due to the activities of later grave-diggers, who, having uncovered the stones, often in fragments, would lay them aside for secondary use by local builders, or, from the eighteenth century onwards, would preserve them for the eyes of the curious visitor. A large number of crosses and cross fragments found in Maughold were preserved due to the scholarly interest of the local vicar, which fired the interest of his son, P. M. C. Kermode (1855-1932). It was the son who extended his interest to cover the whole Island and who, in 1907, published the substantial illustrated catalogue, *Manx Crosses*, which, republished in 1994, has formed the basis of the study of these monuments ever since. It is likely that Kermode's presence in the north of the Island (he lived in Ramsey) may have skewed the number of stones preserved in his time, but there can be no doubt that the importance of nearby Maughold is only slightly exaggerated, for he moved freely about the Island as museum curator and archaeologist, particularly in his later years when he was backed by the authority of the Manx Archaeological Survey, which he set up in 1908 under the enthusiastic chairmanship of the lieutenant-governor, Lord Raglan. (It is noteworthy, however, that no finds of stones are recorded from the churchyards of the two ancient parishes, Arbory and Rushen, in the far south-west of the Island, which Kermode, living some thirty miles away, may have visited less frequently).

The earliest inscribed stones

In the previous chapter it was suggested that the ecclesiastical turbulence which affected western Britain and Ireland in the sixth and seventh century would also have influenced Man; but of this we have no written record, save that found on the stone memorials. The earliest hint of sub-Roman Christian influence on the Island is represented by a 'name-stone' found in the late eighteenth century in the churchyard at Santon (29; fig. 4). The stone is inscribed in Roman characters (in Latin) to the memory of a man called Avitus. Although the inscription is not a specifically Christian formula, it is closely related in style to stones in Christian contexts in Wales, Galloway (Rheged) and, to a lesser extent, in Cornwall and Ireland. The Santon stone is of a type found in other parts of Britain of the sub-Roman period, and is to be dated on the basis of its epigraphy to the early sixth century.

Fig. 4. Santon 29. Inscribed early sixth-century stone from the parish churchyard. Height: 114cm.

A few more elaborate monuments, like the standing pillar from an early burial ground at Knock y Doonee (fig. 3 right), are more explicitly Christian; this stone contains a Christian burial formula *hic iacit* ('here is thrown/laid'), a formula more normally found in both Cornwall and Wales. The form of such stones and this formula seem to have had their origins in Roman Britain and Gaul, having arrived in western Britain and presumably in the Isle of Man with early missionaries in the sixth century. The Knock y Doonee stone is doubly interesting and unusual in that it is also bilingual in Latin and British and is written in two scripts, Roman capitals and ogam. The full Latin inscription, AMMECAT FILIUS ROCAT HIC IACIT (i.e. 'Ammecatus son of Rocatus is laid here'), is repeated and translated without the *hic iacit* formula into the native British language as [E]B[I] CATOS M[A]QI ROC[A]T[OS]). This is rendered in ogam script, an alphabet consisting of twenty incised characters, consisting of short strokes arranged either across or butting onto a median line (fig. 5). At this early stage the Manx language (Goidelic) was related to Welsh and Cumbrian and not to Irish (Brythonic).

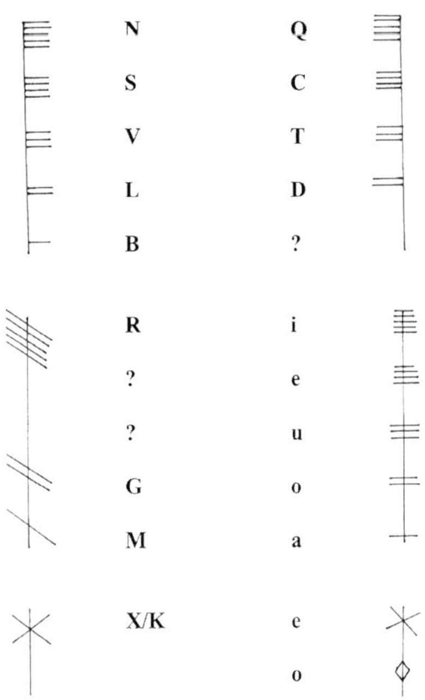

	N		Q	
	S		C	
	V		T	
	L		D	
	B		?	
	R		i	
	?		e	
	?		u	
	G		o	
	M		a	
	X/K		e	
			o	

Fig. 5. A standard ogam alphabet.

Three-hundred and eighty ogam inscriptions are known from Britain, mostly found in western Ireland; others occur chiefly in western Wales, Scotland and Cornwall. Eight have been found on undecorated stones on the Island (nos. 1, 2, 3, 4, 52, 130, 145, 205). The first four of these are primary inscriptions, set up as memorials in burial grounds, and are to be dated to the sixth to seventh centuries; those on stones nos. 52 and 130 are later graffiti; the inscription on no. 145 is probably of twelfth-century date (see p.140) and no. 205, excavated on an early burial site, belongs to the series of 'scholastic' ogams. The inscriptions are simple, sometimes merely recording a single name and patronymic, as on the stone from Knock y Doonee (above). One of two stones from Ballaqueeney (the damaged Rushen 2) records the names of a man and his family or tribe, Bivaidonas, son of Mucoi of the Cunava. The ogam inscriptions on this stone and on the other stone from this site, include a personal-name element, (D)ROATA, which, according to Trench-Jellicoe quoting Ní Catháin, suggests a family relationship between the two people commemorated.

The problem of the keeills

Such early stones are rare and seem, like the sculptured stone crosses of a slightly later period, mostly to have been found in cemeteries of early date, sometimes defined by boundary ditches, in which the dead were often interred in lintel graves. In the period covered by this book, a remarkable number of these cemeteries have produced memorial stones of all periods, often more than one at the same site. Excavation at a number of such sites has produced simple stones with crosses, which acted as grave-markers (best documented at Keeill Vael, Michael; Cronk yn Howe, Lezayre and St Patrick's Isle; see below p.48f).

As was the case in other western parts of Britain, with the exception to some extent of Ireland, these cemeteries are often unrelated to any ecclesiastical structure. On many sites, however, the foundations of small rectangular single-cell stone buildings have been found within the cemetery boundaries, and were identified and labelled with the Manx term *keeill* (cell/chapel) by early antiquarians. Originally such structures were thought to be contemporary with the early crosses and to have functioned as religious buildings; but excavation in the Island and consideration of similar burial-sites in England, Scotland and Wales would suggest that buildings did not appear in the majority of cemeteries until after the period of the erection of the stone crosses, probably during the first half of the eleventh century. It was at this period that ecclesiastical reorganisation led to the erection of what in England have recently been more conveniently labelled 'field churches', buildings which seem to have coincided with the growing ability of the Church to consecrate cemeteries and regulate funerary rites, largely removing cemeteries from the control of families or communities (see below, p.122f, for a fuller discussion of these reforms in a historical context).

A similar pattern seems to have emerged in Man. As Church organisation grew more rigorous, gaining power and influence over the local population, small rectangular buildings began to appear in existing cemeteries.

About 178 such buildings have been recognised in the Island. The term 'keeill' (cell/chapel) implies an ecclesiastical function, but their very number demonstrates that few public offices could have been performed regularly at each one. They would probably have been used for baptisms, marriages and funerals, as well as the occasional mass when a cleric was available. They could also provide the priest with shelter and rough accommodation during his occasional visitation from a central church or other ecclesiastical establishment. Some such central sites presumably developed into parish churches, of which there were ultimately seventeen in the Island (fig. 1), in an administrative ecclesiastical structure which became formalised in the twelfth/thirteenth century. Most keeills cannot be accurately dated (although there is some evidence that a tenth- to twelfth-century building on St Patrick's Isle is a firmly-dated keeill), but they clearly continued to be built or embellished as late as the end of the fourteenth century – as witness the keeill at West Nappin which has a piscina of this date. Incidentally, the east window of this ruined chapel had a lintel consisting of a re-used decorated sculptured stone of the Scandinavian period of settlement of the Island (Jurby 103), implying that the site had been in use as a burial ground in the tenth century, if not earlier.

In the western eremitic tradition isolated keeills may have provided homes for hermits, and may have been earlier than the majority of keeills – such could be the case at Lag ny Keeilley, Patrick. Here the remains of a rectangular building are set on a small platform on a precipitous cliff on the south-west coast of the Island, close to a burial ground in which a number of cross-incised stones were found (see below p.48). The building could have provided domestic accommodation for a hermit on a site very difficult of access. On the other hand it could have been used as a bothy or even as a permanent dwelling of a family who buried their dead there. Buildings at one other site, Maughold, could well belong to an earlier development. Here a small number of rectangular structures survive which could have been built for domestic purposes as the site developed into a major centre of religious life – a monastery (see chapter 3).

Sacred sites

St Patrick's Isle, on the west coast of the Isle of Man, now visible as a castle-crowned islet in a dominant position opposite the medieval town of Peel, has been a centre of ecclesiastical and governmental authority since the eleventh century, and probably much earlier. A cathedral dedicated to

St German was probably first built there in the twelfth century, and abandoned in the eighteenth century. It survives, roofless, a picturesque ruin, together with another disroofed parish church (St Patrick's) of medieval origin, and a round tower of twelfth-century Irish type. The islet was surrounded in the mid-fifteenth century by a curtain wall, which includes a number of substantial interval-towers and other buildings of varying secular and religious functions and date. Excavation has revealed prehistoric activity on the islet, and a number of pre-Viking-Age Christian lintel graves have been uncovered in a cemetery to the north-west of the later cathedral. The ancient parish boundary between Patrick and German still runs between the cathedral and St Patrick's church, where there seems to have been another cemetery, which has been used in the argument that led to the suggestion that St Patrick's was the original cathedral (a theory that has received little support). No burials of early date and no lintel graves have been found in the cemetery of St Patrick's church, but few graves have been excavated here in modern times; the two which were properly excavated were certainly medieval and not stone-lined. A puzzling find from St Patrick's church is a stone (no. 67) which might be identified as part of an early (possibly portable) altar-slab (see below p.47).

A number of graves of Viking-Age date were excavated in the 1980s to the north-west of the cathedral, where the remains of a substantial rectangular building were also found. This has been provisionally identified as a keeill, the foundations of which were overlaid by twelfth-century floors; it was associated with burials dated between the tenth and twelfth century, one of the few such buildings to be properly dated on the Isle of Man.

The sculpture found on St Patrick's Isle is generally of minor importance, although six slabs bearing simple incised linear crosses are associated with the graves excavated to the north of the cathedral. Two fragments (one with a runic inscription), found early in the last century, are certainly of Viking-Age date. Another fragment (no. 195) is of interest as it seems to be either a trial-piece for a complicated interlace pattern of uncertain date or the fragment, possibly incomplete, of a larger stone, re-used in its broken triangular form as a grave-marker. The lack of further examples of early sculpture on the islet may simply be due to the fact that some of the non-excavated memorial slabs were found built into the walls of the cathedral, where many others may have ended up.

The possibility that St Patrick's Isle was the seat of a religious community is emphasised by the twelfth-century round tower (now capped by a

Fig. 6. Tynwald plain before the erection of modern buildings and before the present tree cover. Watercolour by John 'Warwick' Smith, 1795. The picture gives an impression of the site of assemblies of the Manx people from at least the early thirteenth century, and probably earlier. These were accompanied by a fair on Old St John's Day (5 July). The ceremony is now conducted from a stepped mound, perhaps the site of an early burial mound (just visible under a canopy on the left). The early church is seen to the right.

much later crest) of a type found on the site of many religious communities in Ireland. There is thus just a possibility that St Patrick's Isle was at some period in the early Middle Ages a monastic foundation, but for this there is no evidence. In the later period of Scandinavian settlement it was a centre of royal and ecclesiastical power, a status it may well have gained earlier. The sanctity of the place in the pre-Viking age is undoubted; at least it could have been a necropolis served by regular clergy.

One other site in the Isle of Man may have greater significance – not as the seat of a religious community, but rather as a sacred place. This is the traditional site of the Manx national assembly – Tynwald at St Johns (fig. 6) – where there is still an annual meeting of the legislature for the public proclamation of laws passed during the previous year. In earlier times it served a much wider function as a court and in the thirteenth century was described as an 'assembly of the whole Manx people'. Its written history goes back to the Middle Ages, but it is clearly much older – its name, Tynwald, meaning 'assembly field', is of Norse origin – and its use as a site of assembly and authority probably belongs at least to the period of the introduction of formalised Christianity, and quite possibly to a pre-Christian era.

Such sites are known throughout northern Europe (sometimes with similar names – from the Old Norse Þingvǫllr – as Dingwall in northern Scotland, Thingwall, Orkney, Thingvellir in Iceland) and are often associated with burial places of great men or dynasties. By tradition in such places the king or chieftain held court on the burial mound of the founder of a dynasty. At Tynwald the representative of the Lord of Man still sits on the top of a mound on Tynwald Day surrounded by representatives of the Manx people, the public gathering on the plain in front of him. The tiered contour of the mound had probably been shaped for its purpose before the early fifteenth century as the ceremonial centre of such activities. It was probably an ancient burial mound, which has been much interfered with and shaped over the centuries. Although it has never been scientifically excavated, it possibly dates from the Bronze Age (a cist of that date can be seen beside the modern road which runs behind the Tynwald mound), or was the burial place of an important early Scandinavian settler. Indeed, pagan Viking-Age burial mounds have been excavated in various parts of the Island (see below, p.55).

There are possible traces of at least two other mounds on the promontory which forms the Tynwald Plain, which, together with the Tynwald mound itself, are associated with discrete burial-places for the dead, sometimes in lintel graves. The date of these mounds and many of the graves is not known. A single piece of a decorated, rune-inscribed cross-slab (German 107) of the early Scandinavian period, found on the site of the church, is evidence of an earlier Christian burial ground. Small finds of Viking-Age date found in some of the graves demonstrate its use as a burial place in that period. The presence of the dead, centred in some cases on the burial mound of an ancestral ruler or chieftain, seen in Scandinavia and in its overseas settlements, gave to central sites like Tynwald a sense of mystery and awe. The presence of ancestral burials provided for a perceived continuity of wisdom and authority. Thus such places became important in both secular and ecclesiastical discussion and decision on the occasion of an assembly of the people. There is no reason why such assemblies should not have been held before the coming of the Scandinavians – indeed this is highly probable. It is not, however, difficult to interpret this site as a seat of power at the geographical centre of the Island, rooted in a secular and religious past, as a place of judgement presided over by chieftains and priests, at a period when the ecclesiastical hierarchy at the borders of Christendom was only roughly defined.

CHAPTER 3

The monastery at Maughold and pre-Scandinavian monuments in the Island

Maughold

HOWEVER we look at the early Church in the Isle of Man, it is clear that the only significant, exclusively Christian establishment which can be recognised today is the monastery at Maughold. The remains still to be seen on St Patrick's Isle and at Tynwald Hill, outlined in the previous chapter, demonstrate that while both sites have real public significance, they are simply numinous places where secular and ecclesiastical power met. A half-hearted attempt to identify one phase of the important, partially excavated, multi-period site at Ronaldsway as 'a minor monastery' of eighth- or ninth-century date, is poorly argued and cannot be sustained. The isolated and precipitous cliff-side site of Lag ny Keeilley, Patrick, where graves and ten simple grave-markers bearing linear crosses have been found, and which also has the remains of a rectangular building, may, as suggested above (p.18), reflect the eremitical tradition of early Christianity in the west of Britain. But this is not proven, and indeed it is the only site of this type on the Island, the function of which is postulated purely on the basis of its isolated topographical situation. It cannot, however, be seen as a site of major influence in the Island's Christian story. So we must turn to Maughold.

The history of the Christian site at Maughold is only fleetingly visible in written sources. References to it and to its patron saint in Irish sources and in a supposed thirteenth-century Papal Bull are of doubtful value; while references to miraculous acts of its patronal saint, Machutus, in an entry for 1156 in the *Chronicle of the Kings of Man and the Isles* (the last entries in which seem to have been made in 1316), have now been dismissed as later interpolations. The first written record of the site (*Kirkemaghald*) is in 1302 in the *Register of the Priory of St Bees*.

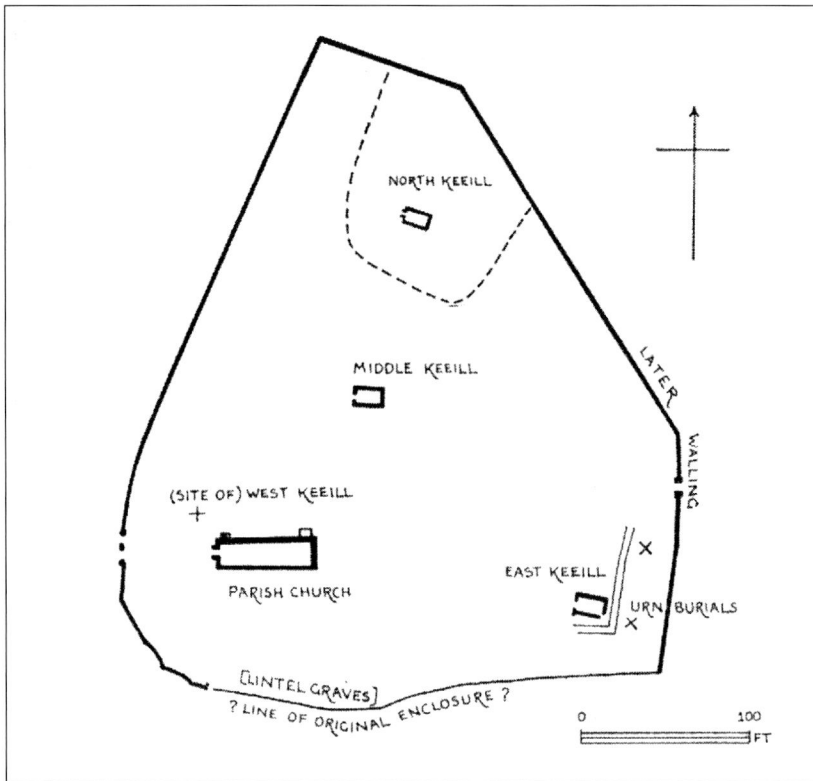

*Fig. 7. Maughold churchyard. Survey by P. M.C. Kermode,
modified by A.C. Thomas. The 'keeills' marked on the map
should more properly be labelled as 'cells'. Evidence for the
presence of lintel graves on the southern boundary depends
solely on this plan. Although unrecorded elsewhere, it is not
unlikely that such graves were found here.*

The identity of a monastic community at Maughold depends almost
exclusively on the carved stones and other archaeological remains found in
the present-day parish churchyard (fig. 7). These provide clear evidence of
burials from the early Christian and Scandinavian periods and also of a
measure of monastic learning. Features of the present parish church date
back to the twelfth century; indeed the church itself might have been built
on the site of an older building. The church lies within a large churchyard
which also encloses a well and the remains of four surviving rectangular
buildings. These have for many years been labelled as keeills, but, as

Kermode earlier indicated, they might better be described as cells. They survive only as wall-footings rebuilt in the nineteenth century. The church-yard is large. When first recorded by the Ordnance Survey in 1869 it measured 3.5 acres, i.e. 1.41ha. Since then slight alterations to the boundary wall have brought into use a little more space for graves to the north, while the pathway on the east side has been straightened. The irregular shape of the graveyard is clearly the result of alteration and modification over the centuries, during which much of the enclosed area has been filled with graves. Excavation by the Manx Archaeological Survey in 1915 within the present wall revealed a substantial bank and possible external ditch in the south-east corner of the graveyard, near the East Keeill. Clearly of some age, this could represent part of the original monastic precinct. At the time of the Survey's recording it was recollected that the ditch had extended in a line within the full length of the present graveyard wall. The bank is no longer visible, while the presence of modern graves prohibits further archaeological investigation of the bank and ditch.

As mentioned, there is little likelihood that the so-called keeills at Maughold functioned as chapels before the eleventh century. Indeed, tenth-century memorial slabs built into the walls of at least one of them, and the presence of lintel graves below the level of the walls in the north keeill, indicate that, while they cannot necessarily have been part of the original monastery, they may well have had an ecclesiastical use before the establishment of the parochial system, probably in the thirteenth century. But it is the presence of a number of early inscriptions on the sculptured stones on the site that most strongly stresses its identity as a monastic foundation. Maughold must be seen as one of the relatively few British monasteries to have developed a local sculptural tradition and to have been the centre of production of the crosses themselves. This fact has been emphasised by Bailey for the whole of the Irish Sea region, in relation to specific concentrations of sculpture in north-west England and south-west Scotland in the pre-Viking period.

Early inscribed stones from Maughold

The most striking and convincing argument for the presence of a monastic foundation at Maughold is provided by a Latin inscription in an uncial script (characters of the rounded form seen in manuscripts written in Britain and Ireland in the seventh to early ninth century), which was found in the churchyard in 1948. The inscription, in a rectangle in the middle of

Fig. 8. Maughold 169. The insular minuscule inscription.

a ring-headed cross fragment (169, fig. 8), reads: '[in the name of] Jesus Christ, Branhui brought water to this place' (a stone-lined culvert recorded on the site may relate to this inscription). It seems possible that the text was delineated by a scribe using a book-hand; it is not a stone-mason's epigraphic script. Another uncial inscription in a book-hand may be seen on the shoulder of the substantial granite slab (Maughold 69; fig. 9), from Port y Vullen, very close to the monastic site at Maughold. The inscription (fig. 10) reads *crux guriat* ('the cross of Guriat'), implying that the cross was carved at the local granite source of the monastery, in memory of a man with a Celtic, presumably Welsh, name cognate with Gwyriad. The sophistication of the lettering on these two stones and the fact (recorded in the elegant Latin inscription on no. 169) that some sort of aqueduct had been

Fig. 9. Maughold 69. Granite cross from Port y Vullen. First recorded before 1841 in the middle of a field, it was later moved to the roadside, and finally transferred to the cross-house in Maughold churchyard. Kermode suggested that it came from a burial site, Ballaterson keeill. Height 132cm.

Fig. 10. Insular uncial inscription on the shoulder of Maughold 69 (fig. 9). Drawing by P. M. C. Kermode.

Fig. 11. Maughold 41. In the top right-hand corner is the Greek letter omega *(ω). The photograph was taken c.1910, but the character has now almost completely worn away. Height: 55cm.*

constructed at Maughold, implies the presence of a high-status monastic community in the eighth century.

Further sophistication is demonstrated by the presence on another slab (Maughold 41; fig. 11), in the angle between the ringed cross-head and the top right-hand corner of the slab, of the Greek letter *ω* (*omega*). This refers to the passage in the Book of Revelations (1:8), 'I am the Alpha and the Omega, says the Lord God'. The letter *alpha* was presumably inscribed on the (now missing) left-hand corner of the stone. The two characters appear in variant forms on Irish monastic sites, in manuscripts, and on a small number of later memorial stones at St David's, in south-west Wales, as well as in associated places in the immediate region of this important Welsh ecclesiastical centre.

No other formal uncial inscriptions are known from the Island, although

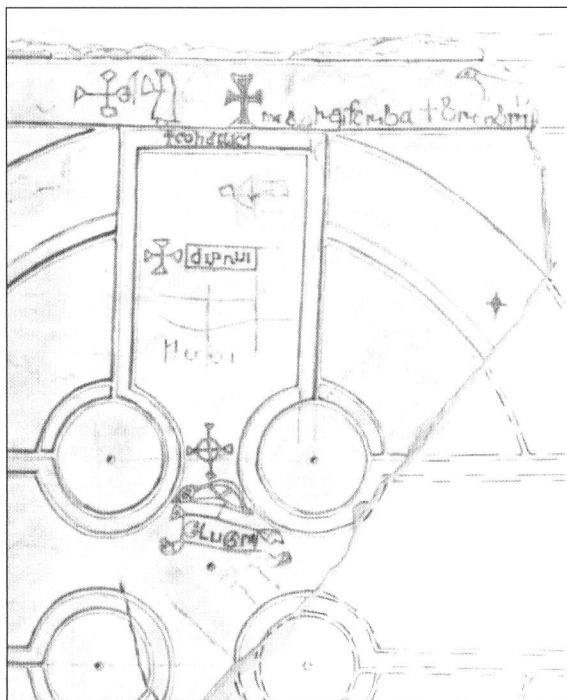

Fig. 12. Bride 52. The stone has a number of graffiti, including names in insular uncial. From an early burial ground at Ballavarkish. Height: 58cm.

a number of names inscribed in uncial characters do occur as graffiti on the fragment of a slab from a keeill site at Ballavarkish, Bride (52; fig. 12), which Macalister characterised rather unfairly as looking 'like the work of ancient schoolboys'. The graffiti must, however, be taken more seriously; they consist of a number of graffiti of crosses and figures together with six personal names executed in insular uncial. The names appear to be in different hands, the two clearest names being *Condilici* and *Diprui*. One inscription identifies a scribe (*scriba*). Although his name is difficult to decipher, it is written in a fairly competent hand and may be read as MAILOR-EI (see below pp.131-2). This is the only occurrence in the Isle of Man in the pre-Scandinavian period of a named scribe. Another graffito of Christ's name is roughly incised on the back of Maughold 169.

Much more important, however, is the most intriguing stone of this early

Fig. 13. Maughold 47. Note the hooked crosses:
monogram of the name of Christ (the Greek
letters chi and rho). Height: 68cm.

Fig. 14. Seal-die of
an Anglo-Saxon
bishop (below), found
at Eye, Suffolk.
(British Museum).

group from Maughold (47; fig. 13), which has a number of sometimes
rather blundered (i.e. misunderstood) transcriptions or damaged characters. At the top of its decorated face is a roundel formed of three incised
lines, in the centre of which is a hexafoil surrounded by a partly-damaged

Fig. 15. Malew 164. Possible re-used altar-slab from the cemetery at Ronaldsway. Note the three tau-crosses, representing the crosses on Calvary. Height: 63.5cm.

and blundered Latin inscription, written in a mixture of insular letter forms. This has been read from the top as XPI NO[mi]NE ITSPLI EPPS DE I[NN]SVLI ('In the name of Christ, *Itspli* bishop of the island'); after what is probably an ampersand the text reverses to read from the damaged edge at the top CBAT [&] G, the meaning of which is obscure. Below the roundel are two linear crosses with serif-like terminals. The serifs at the top right-hand side of each cross are extended to form a hook. Hooked crosses of this type are a well-known derivative of the Greek *chi-rho* monogram for the name of Christ (the Christogram). This is explained in the inscription which runs from the stem of one cross to the other and reads IN IHU XPI NOMINE / CRUCIS XPI IMAGENEM ('In the name of Christ, an image of the cross of Christ').

The roundel almost certainly represents the seal-impression of a bishop, whose name is obscure. It may be compared with the image on the striking-face of the ninth-century seal-die of a Bishop Æthelwald (probably the bishop, *c.*845-70, of the short-lived see of Dunwich in Suffolk), which was found 200m from the nearby Anglo-Saxon monastery of Eye (fig. 14). The similarity of layout of the two roundels is remarkable, even down to the related ornament in the central panel. The two crosses on the stone (of which another example, without the hooks, is to be seen on no. 48) might indicate a somewhat earlier date than the seal-die. Interesting parallels in this context are the hooked equal-armed crosses within roundels on three sixth-century inscribed stones from Kirkmadrine, in Galloway, one of which records the epitaph HIC IACENT S(AN)C(T)I ET PRAECIPUI SACER DOTES IDES VIVENTIUS ET MAVORIUS ('Here lie the holy and eminent sacerdotes [i.e. 'senior priests'], Ides, Viventius and Mavorius').

The form of the crosses on the Maughold stones, with their long shafts and marked serifs, may be compared to a cross without a hook on another stone from Maughold (48) and to the three *tau*-crosses (i.e. T-shaped) on the slab from Ronaldsway (164; fig. 15, see also below, p.115). Crosses with long shafts and serifed terminals are to be found on stones from two or three sites in Galloway (for example at Laggangarn), while in Ireland they are to be seen, for instance, on stones from Gallen Priory, Co. Offaly. Similar crosses occur on the seventh-century wooden portable altar from the coffin of St Cuthbert (died 687), found in the saint's grave in Durham cathedral.

If the dates of the Gallowegian and Northumbrian objects are correct, it is possible that stone no. 47 is a relic of an early phase of a monastic institution at Maughold (possibly even in the seventh century); but there remains the problem of the identity of the bishop and of his see. There is no evidence of a territorial bishop in the Isle of Man in the ninth century (the date of the Suffolk seal to which the roundel has been compared), although it is not impossible that such a see existed even though it is only documented on a single stone. But such an assumption must be queried, particularly as the monastery of Maughold – literate in Latin and (on admittedly slender evidence, as will be shown) possibly in English – was a sophisticated religious settlement of a type documented elsewhere in the British Isles, quite capable of supporting a learned community and an ecclesiastical hierarchy.

Such a community was the monastery at Whithorn in Galloway, easily visible from the Isle of Man and only a short distance from it. Traditionally founded by St Ninian, a Briton who came from Rome and built a church there (*candida casa*, 'the white house'), it seems to have been the seat of a Northumbrian bishopric from the late seventh century, its boundary with Dumfries in the east being the River Nith. The monastery of Whithorn itself has produced few stones of this period, although there is a striking early stone – the inscribed 'Petrus' stone – which must date to the sixth century and could be compared loosely with Maughold 47. But, as has been shown, there are a number of memorial stones from Kirkmadrine, some 20km from Whithorn, which, with others from the immediate region, can be loosely paralleled with the Maughold stone. Later, in the late ninth and tenth century, a school of sculpture was established in the Galloway region, one example of which was at Whithorn. This may have influenced the sculptors of the Island, and was certainly in tune with the general design of sculpture in the Isle of Man (see below, p.72). Contact between Maughold and Whithorn would have been relatively easy by sea, particularly if either monastery, like Iona, owned a boat and employed sailors.

The history of Whithorn, as with so many religious foundations on the edges of the Northumbrian kingdom, is complicated, and goes back into the early period (sixth century) of the 'Celtic' Church. Could it be that the monastery at Maughold was founded from Whithorn? There is no evidence at all that such was the case, but it is not inherently impossible, for Ninian himself, so tradition says, indulged in missionary activity, to such an extent that he is sometimes known as the apostle of the Picts. Why then should he not have ventured to Man as well? Whatever the case, the fact that there was a bishopric in the nearby ancient foundation of Whithorn in the seventh and eighth century might have led the cleric in charge of Maughold to assume or be given the title of bishop in imitation of his more important brother across the water in Galloway; the inscription on Maughold 47 ('bishop of the island') may refer to an early period of Maughold's history as a monastery. Ecclesiastical titles in the western British church at this time were often used in indiscriminate fashion. The word 'abbot' rarely appeared; more common were such titles as 'bishop' or *sacerdos* (a word meaning 'priest', often signifying one of senior rank), as on the stone from Kirkmadrine (above, p.32), which were often used in both Wales and Ireland to signify the head of a *monasterium*. The terminology of the ecclesiastical hierarchy in this period is so complicated that for the non-specialist it is perhaps wisest to take the line proposed by John Blair:

> …if we concentrate on structures and functions rather than striving to recognise invisible boundaries between clerical and monastic, we can observe an important development: the emergence of big ecclesiastical settlements which might house bishops, abbots, priests, deacons and monks in a variety of combinations.

Fig. 16. Maughold 42.
The inscription is in
Anglo-Saxon runes.
Height: 111cm.

Thus it is reasonable to describe Maughold in the period before the Scandinavian settlement as a monastery, the house of a largish and sophisticated Christian community, probably founded in the late sixth or early seventh century, and led by a cleric of some standing, probably with the title of bishop; an establishment in touch with the major monastic communities of England, Scotland and Ireland.

Outside influences

The Anglo-Saxon (i.e. Northumbrian) elements present on the stones at Maughold have received little attention; but such connections do exist, even if they are exiguous. The presence of what might be the carved reproduction of an episcopal seal on the stone from Maughold (47; fig. 13) may be indicative of Anglo-Saxon influence. Better known, and most definitely derived from Northumbria, are two simple memorial stones with inscribed ringed crosses. Within the ring of one is the name **blagcmon** (Maughold 42; fig.16) in Anglo-Saxon runes. On the second stone (no. 43), of which only a fragment survives, four characters of the same name …**gmon**, also in Anglo-Saxon runes, now remain within what is left of an incised ring. The name *Blagcmon* (modern Blackman), is reasonably common in Old English. The stones were probably the head- and foot-stones of the grave of a Northumbrian, presumably carved or commissioned by a countryman at the monastery.

The arms of the incised cross on this slab are filled with a closed three-looped interlace pattern known as a triquetra, a typical decorative element of the whole Hiberno-Saxon area (England and western and northern Britain in the early Christian period). Triquetra-filled cross-arms also appear in low relief on a slab from a keeill site at Balnahowe, Santon, no. 95. These compass-drawn crosses with triquetra-filled arms (and a much smaller plain linear-encircled cross drawn below the main symbol on Maughold 42, now no longer visible) are formed of conjoined chords of a circle, a motif which also occurs, for example, on the fragmentary stone no. 43. The same construction on another incised stone from Maughold, no. 46, has, below the cross, an incised roundel bordering a hexafoil of similar form to that found within the main roundel on Maughold 47. Close parallels to these compass-drawn crosses, with or without the filler in the arms, are frequently found in Ireland, and, occasionally, in western Scotland (notably on the 'St Peter Stone' from Whithorn).

This was a period of wide-ranging international religious contacts. British Christians (presumably numbering among them those native to the Isle of Man) were influenced initially from the Church in Gaul, possibly through the medium of continentally-trained missionaries and priests who established ecclesiastical institutions which were to be deeply influenced by Rome, and more so as a group of English bishops began to impose a Roman discipline on an irregular, sometimes feuding, native church in the west. The traces of Latinity observed at Maughold indicate its position in the mainstream of the development of Northumbrian Christianity.

Fig. 17. Maughold 51. Fragmentary panel showing the
remains of an incised ringed-cross. Height: 38cm.

Maughold crosses of the pre-Viking Age without incidental decoration

A number of stones from Maughold (41 [fig. 11], 42 [fig. 16], 43, 46, 48, 51 [fig. 17], 169, and 190), some of which have been discussed above, have sharply-incised unembellished crosses (some formed of chords of a circle, others of straight lines), which are sometimes emphasised by careful pecking. This type of delineation is paralleled in Ireland, Wales, Scotland and Northumbria. Most of the Manx examples have carefully-drawn ring-crosses, equal-armed and made up of compass-drawn chords of circles; two bear a compass-drawn hexafoil or 'marigold' pattern within a circle (e.g. nos. 46 and 190), while on no. 51 (fig. 17) the arms of the ringed-cross with straight arms extend across the enclosing circle to meet a double-contoured rectilinear incised frame. On Maughold 42 and 46 various variants of the compass-drawn figures occur separately outside the main ring-cross.

Only at Ballavarkish, Bride (52; fig. 12) and Ronaldsway 164 (fig. 15) do other examples of such carefully and accurately-drawn crosses occur.

The sharply-incised slabs are most easily paralleled in Galloway and the Western Isles of Scotland, with a few outliers in the east, although none of the crosses on these slabs are enclosed in double-contoured rectilinear frames. The same may be said of the rare examples in Wales (for example at St Teilo's Church, Merthyr Mawr, Glamorgan). Related stones of similar design are rare in Northumbria, but on the site of a monastery at Hartlepool, on the eastern coast of Northumbria, which was founded from the western 'Celtic' church, a number of rectangular limestone plaques related in form to those on the Island, have been excavated. The crosses framed by crisply-incised lines are still clearly seen, because many may well have laid face-up on the surface of graves, where they were soon obscured by turf and only revealed by modern excavation. The 400 stones found at Clonmacnoise, Co. Offaly, and in smaller numbers at a few other monastic sites elsewhere in Ireland, are practically all smaller and more elaborate than the Maughold group, and include a large number of formal memorial inscriptions in insular uncial. Many are recumbent slabs, often with an inscription recording the name of the dead person, and, although largely different in style, they do provide parallels to the Manx series, particularly in the form of the cross on Maughold 53. No stones of either type have, however, been found in north-west England.

Some of the Manx slabs have been interpreted as altar-frontals, particularly nos. 41 (fig. 11) and 51 from Maughold (fig. 17), 52 from Ballavarkish, Bride (fig. 12), and 164 from Ronaldsway (fig. 15), although in most cases this may be an incorrect supposition. Their dimensions do, however, suggest that they could have belonged to some form of composite monument. The fragmentary inscribed Branhui stone from Maughold (169; fig. 8) – which was presumably part of a composite monument – should be included in this group. Unfortunately all these Maughold stones which, together with the Ballavarkish stone, could be by the same hand, are too fragmentary to be so identified with any confidence.

Save for no. 164 (fig. 15), which comes from Ronaldsway in the south of the Island, all these stones are carved in well-bedded, smooth-surfaced mudstone, beautifully and accurately laid out. The Ronaldsway stone, however, appears to be complete. It has a different, coarser texture (it is of microgranite, medium-grained except for a thin, darker, fine-grained outer layer). Possibly an erratic, its texture accounts for its less sharply-cut

Fig. 18. Marown 6 and 7, 'St Patrick's Chair'. There are incised linear crosses on the two upright stones on the left. The height of the tallest stone is 188cm.

appearance by comparison with the normal Manx mudstone. The design, while rather different from that on the other stones in this group, is clearly related to them. Fortunately this stone was excavated, if in a very amateurish fashion, in association with two early lintel graves. The stone formed the headstone of two graves laid side-by-side, with prominent corner-posts at the south-east and south-west corners. The graves were covered by slabs, and it would seem that the head and foot-stone and at least one lateral stone formed an open 'chest', which was filled, either at the time of the inhumation or later, with white pebbles. At first thought to be a secondarily-used 'altar-slab' (or *mensa*), it seems more likely that it is in its original position, and, if so, could possibly have been, with the rest of the structure, part of a *leacht* (an outdoor memorial platform or altar of a type found in Ireland) as possibly represented by 'St Patrick's Chair' in the Island (nos. 6 and 7; fig. 18), which may, however, be an early nineteenth-century folly. But, more probably, the Ronaldsway stone is part of a 'corner-post' shrine (in form not unlike a late medieval tomb-chest) placed

Fig. 19. Standing posts, probably the corner-posts of a shrine or tomb. From 1935 emergency excavations at Ronaldsway, Malew. The unexcavated box behind them was apparently a box tomb which overlaid a skeleton.

over the grave of a founder or some other important man. Such a post was in fact found at one corner of the structure, which indeed protected a skeleton (fig. 19). Such 'corner-post shrines' (usually more elaborately constructed) are known in the Pictish areas of Scotland, where composite monuments are more commonly found, most famously at St Andrews, but are apparently unknown elsewhere in the British Isles. It is not impossible that some of the fragmentary mudstone slabs with incised designs from Maughold and Bride were also part of corner-post or box-shrines like that found at Ronaldsway.

One of these fragmentary slabs, from a burial ground (and presumably a later keeill site) at Ballavarkish, Bride (52; fig. 12) has a face incised with a well-constructed, double-contoured ring-headed cross with armpits made up of three-quarter circles. On it, as has been shown above, are a number of graffiti of crosses and figures, together with six names executed in insular uncial of eighth/ninth-century date. Similar graffiti have recently been found on stones excavated at a chapel site at Inchmarnock, Bute, which are similarly dated. All these graffiti are generally accepted to be of the eighth/ninth century, which is important in that it helps to place the slab in the period before the Scandinavian settlement of Man. This is chronologically useful in relation to other ring-headed crosses of the same form and construction found on the Island.

The carvers of the group of finely-incised stones from Maughold were influenced in different ways by monastic elements of the church in Ireland and Pictland, but perhaps more particularly, as demonstrated by the Hartlepool slabs, by the newly-established Northumbrian church, far away on the eastern coast of England.

As has been shown, names cut on two of the simple incised Maughold crosses (42, fig.16; and no. 43) are inscribed in Anglo-Saxon runes, which demonstrates contact with Northumbria, memorialising a man with an English name, inscribed by a man with a competence in the script – presumably another Englishman. How many of their countrymen were members of this community (or simply temporary visitors to it) cannot be estimated, but, as will be shown, the Northumbrian contact is indicated by the ornament of a number of crosses, probably of a later period, which is clearly related to that of stone sculpture in England (pp.62 and 67).

The Manx stones demonstrate, however modestly, a degree of literacy and learning on the Island, and provide evidence of a church in contact with the world outside. They also indicate the development of the monastery at Maughold during the eighth and ninth century as it derived inspiration from the religious communities in the surrounding lands.

Plain crosses in low relief

Another group of rather more elaborate stones of this period, mostly from Maughold, seem to be related to contemporary stones from Scotland (nos. 53, 54, 55, 56, 57, 68, 70, 90, 91, 96). All are embellished with a cross carved in low relief, but, unlike these contemporaries, without interlace or other ornament; many are of granite. They are paralleled at two other sites on the Island, at Lonan (71, fig.22; 75, 76 and 77) and Braddan (63), and must be considered as part of this series, which conceivably may have been carved by sculptors from the workshop of the monastery at Maughold. Few of these stones are complete, most being head fragments; but Maughold 68 (fig. 20), which belongs to a rather coarser bed of mudstone than is usually found at this site, is complete. The top of the stone is slightly curved. On both faces is a ring-headed cross, the two crosses being of similar design. The shafts expand towards the foot and are defined by

Fig. 20. Maughold 68.
Plain ringed cross with a
central boss in low relief.
Height: 132cm.

rolled borders. The arms extend for a short distance across the ring to reach the edge of the stone. The cross-heads are slightly raised above the ring. There is a boss in the middle of each head and the background of the crosses and the armpits are cut in intaglio. Cross no. 57 is not dissimilar, while the surviving heads of most of the rest of the group, although only carved on one face, are often more definitely rounded and are generally related in form to no. 68.

A rather grander version of this design is the granite cross Maughold 69, a stone with the Latin inscription reading *crux guriat* (figs. 9 and 10; above, pp. 27-8). It came not from the monastic site itself, but from a hedge in the roadside at Port y Vullen, immediately above the beach where the stone was quarried. (Kermode suggested that it had originally been moved from the site of a keeill at Ballaterson). Another cross, from Ballalheaney, Lonan (71; fig. 22), is clearly related to the group, but has features which are possibly later (see below).

Unlike most Maughold stones, which were carved in the fine-grained local mudstone, Maughold 53, 69, 90 and 91 are of granite, almost certainly taken from the dyke which outcrops on the nearby beach at Port y Vullen. Another much smaller stone cross, Maughold 57, from a now untraceable keeill to the north of Ballaglass Mill, is of siltstone; but, as it was found at some distance from Port y Vullen, possibly came from a more local quarry. The granite crosses of this series from Maughold are all carefully carved. No. 90 lacks the ring at the cross-head. No. 91 is unique in that the foot of the cross terminates in a broad carved ring framing an outlined cross, the symbolism of which might relate to the 'cross on orb' motif that appears on Merovingian coins, symbolising Christ's sovereignty. This feature is rare in western Britain, but is paralleled at Llanychaer, Pembrokeshire. It is possible that these stones were all the work of a local mason, perhaps a member of the Maughold community, working at or near the granite dyke. Could the impressive stone no. 69, with its inscription in memory of Guriat, have marked the grave of the sculptor, inscribed by a literate friend on a stone he had finished before his death? An interesting sandstone parallel to the undecorated Manx stone no. 69 comes from Rosemarkie, Ross and Cromarty, in the north of Pictland, which is probably the end of a shrine tomb or other composite monument, like those in the mudstone group from Maughold discussed above.

The plain crosses in low relief from Maughold form a remarkably consistent group and are clearly the product of the same workshop. Most stones are roughly rectangular in shape, but Maughold 70, which is of lime-stone, probably from deposits in Castletown Bay in the south of the Island (a stone which is perhaps easier to trim), has a ringed cross-head which protrudes from the sides of the slab, and a rectangular panel at its base. The other face (the back) outlines the cross-head and the panel below it with a single bead, a feature which, with the more elaborate treatment of Maughold 68 (fig. 20) foreshadows the treatment of the slabs (being carved on both faces) of the Scandinavian period. All the other stones in this group, with these two exceptions, whatever the stone from which they were carved, were executed in low relief on one face and are embellished within the carefully-contoured stones with ringed cross-heads and long main stems. The contours are emphasised by an engraved inner outline. Some have elaborate base panels: the cross on Maughold 90, for example, has a step with a rolled border continuing from the sides of the cross; another (Maughold 91), as we have noted, has a double contoured ring at the base containing an equal-armed cross. Two crosses in this group have promi-nent bosses at the ends and/or in the middle of the cross-head (no. 69 and the atypical no. 59).

A Pictish influence

Most important for comparative purposes, however, is Maughold 96 (fig. 21), which, being of laminated fine-grained sandstone and mudstone, has weathered badly. Carved in low relief, it has a simple ring-headed cross with no border. Its long shaft runs to the bottom of the stone. In the pan-els on either side of the shaft are two hooded and seated figures, facing each other across the shaft. On the basis of related scenes elsewhere they are generally agreed to represent the fourth-century fathers of the Church, Paul and Antony, in the desert where they were fed by ravens (not present here), a story recorded in the fourth century by Jerome in his life of Paul, the first hermit. Below these figures on either side of the shaft are balanced panels delineating in the upper register a now rather worn horse and rider, below which are single animals (that on the left appears to be a pug-like dog, that on the right is now hardly visible). Trench-Jellicoe has pointed out that panels on either side of the shaft, just below the head, appear to have enclosed inscriptions, now completely worn away.

A good parallel to the Paul and Antony scene is to be found on a Pictish sandstone slab from Fowlis Wester, Perthshire, which has the same plain, seated, hooded figures on either side of a cross. Here, however, the stone

Fig. 21. Maughold 96. In this more-than-a-century-old photograph, details of the ornament of its now much weather-worn surface are clear. Under the cross-head are representations of the early fathers, Paul and Antony, in the desert. Below are traces of a hunting scene. Height: 142cm.

is much more highly decorated; interlace fills the body of the cross, together with elaborate symbolic figures. Other examples of this scene, sometimes together with the ravens, are to be found elsewhere in Pictland and in one panel of a single Northumbrian monument, the famous late seventh- to eighth-century cross from Ruthwell, Dumfriesshire. It is possible to overemphasize the Pictish parallels to this scene, as the scene was also popular elsewhere, although on the Irish High Crosses it is placed in a more incidental fashion. The Pictish versions, however, occur (not as in Ireland and on the Ruthwell cross) on free-standing crosses, but generally on rectangular slabs with rounded heads similar in form to the Manx series of granite stones.

The animals at the base of the Paul and Antony slab from Maughold also have connections with Pictland and Ireland, in that they depict a (now much worn) stylised hunting scene, but one which will be encountered again on later Manx crosses (below, p.118). Other elements which might be Pictish are the bosses found on Maughold nos. 59, 68 and 69, which were probably inspired by the sometimes elaborately-carved bosses found on slabs and crosses from mainland Scotland and the Western Isles; although perhaps not too much emphasis should be placed on this parallel, as similar bosses also occur in Ireland. The corner-post shrine/grave from the important Ronaldsway site (above, p.32) is, however, presumably based on an idea imported from Pictland, as such structures are unknown elsewhere in the British Isles.

A Pictish connection is further illustrated by a number of stones in other parts of the Island – particularly a group of crosses from the parish of Lonan, which are clearly related to the plain, undecorated cross-slabs from Maughold discussed above. One such is particularly intriguing: the cross from Ballalheaney, Glenroy, Lonan 71 (fig. 22), which was moved to the present parish churchyard in the nineteenth century from a possible keeill site. It is one of a group of four stones from Lonan which have plain contoured ring-heads in low relief; nos. 75 and 76 are of a fine-grained local sandstone laminated with mudstone, while no. 77 is of a local igneous rock, possibly gabbro. The circular heads protrude beyond the straight sides of the slab. Only fragments of the heads of 75 and 77 survive. Most of 76 is intact, but the stone is badly fractured, and repaired below the head. The short plain shaft stands on a double rolled moulding above a damaged foot.

Lonan 71 (fig. 22) is of the same form, but at the foot of the cross the plain beaded border on each side is produced to form an out-turned spiral.

Fig. 22. Lonan 71.
From Ballalheaney. The
shaft is decorated with a
motif not unlike the
'mirror' motif common
in Pictish art. The
elaborate spirals at the
foot of the cross are
related to similar
features on memorial
stones of the Scandi-
navian series, and the
stone must, therefore, be
of late ninth or early
tenth-century date.
Height: 188cm.

On the shaft of the cross is a figure reasonably close in form to the mirror symbol which occurs frequently on Pictish sculpture. The treatment at the foot of the cross, with its out-turned (rather incompetently executed) spirals, is seen quite frequently in a similar position on a number of other cross-slabs on the Island which are of Scandinavian date (e.g. fig. 55), which are discussed below (pp. 72, 115). This otherwise almost unembellished cross from Lonan is clearly related to the Maughold granite group discussed above; the spirals at the base, however, must be an early expression of a feature developed on the highly-decorated Scandinavian crosses (like that in fig. 55) and should probably, therefore, be dated to the early tenth century. Most of the other crosses must date from the eighth century until the initial settlement of the Island by Scandinavians in the early tenth century.

Another intriguing Pictish parallel is provided by a cut-down stone (seen by some as part of a cross with a curved head), possibly an altar-slab, from St Patrick's church on St Patrick's Isle (67). Of local medium-grained greywacke (i.e. grey sandstone found locally), it features a cross in low relief embellished with five incised linear crosslets. It is, however, much cut down, and its original shape cannot be retrieved. Contemporary altar-slabs typically have five incised crosses, best seen, for example, on the wooden portable altar from the late seventh-century Northumbrian coffin of St Cuthbert (above, p.32). Another stone from a keeill site at Ballaglonney, Rushen (no. 66; fig. 23), is of similar design, save that it is formed as a cross with sunken irregular squares dividing its four arms. It is clearly a standing memorial cross, with five incised crosslets around the cross-head, figures which commonly refer to Christ's pauses on the Via Dolorosa.

In their use of relief these two slabs are paralleled by the elaborately-carved fragment of a rectangular slab bearing a cross in relief from Tarbat, Ross and Cromarty (probably from the monastery recently excavated at Portmahomack), where the five crosses on the head are not incised but carved in relief. A small number of stones embellished like no. 66 with four or five incised additional crosses are known from Ireland (from monastic sites like Clonmacnoise, Co. Offaly, and Ardmore, Co. Waterford). With a few exceptions, these examples, together with a much-damaged slab from Papa Stronsay, Orkney, are usually considered to be the centres of altar-tables (originally perhaps set in a wooden or stone plate), and have been compared with the St Patrick's Isle stone. However, they are generally much smaller than the Manx and Pictish examples, which are almost certainly parts of standing crosses.

*Fig. 23. Rushen 66. Cross-slab from
Ballaglonney. The inscribed crosses
presumably represent the five stations of the
Cross on the Via Dolorosa. Height: 96cm.*

Simple grave-markers

Before considering the more elaborately embellished sculptured slabs of
the period of the Scandinavian settlement of the island, attention should be
turned to the long series of simple, mostly roughly-carved, grave-markers.
Such stones are comparatively rare at Maughold. Many are simply linear
incised crosses, often cut with a sharp tool on smallish (30-40cm in length),
usually triangular, pieces of stone (the pointed end of which could thus easily be driven into the ground). They have most frequently been found during excavations at keeill sites, as, for example, at the possible hermitage at
Lag ny Keeilley, Patrick (nos. 9, 10, 174, 181, 201, 202 and 203) and at

Cronk yn How, Lezayre (nos. 150, 151, 152, 153, 154 and 157), as well as on St Patrick's Isle. Interestingly, all the grave-markers at Keeil Vael, Michael (183-80), were built into the walls of the keeill, or were located as to imply such; a position which would imply a pre-tenth/eleventh-century date. It would be tedious to list all such crosses, which are stylistically impossible to date, although some were found in the walls of keeills – for example, Patrick 15 (from Lag ny Keeilley), which formed the sill of the window at the east end. The simple linear cross is much in evidence among the grave-markers and is sometimes given emphasis by outlining its outside contour (e.g. Cronk yn How 151, 153 and 156), sometimes including a ring where the arms cross. Many of the cross-slabs are little more than scratched attempts at depicting such variants as panelled and ring-headed crosses. Some are more competently incised than others, some are more carefully outlined (e.g. Maughold 39), others are merely very clumsily carved (e.g. Marown 50). One of the Cronk yn How stones (no. 158) has a lightly- scratched regular marigold pattern like those found on grander stones from Maughold (fig. 13); in other contexts it might be labelled as a 'trial-piece' or 'motif-piece'.

Parallels to these various unsophisticated crosses have been found in all the non-Anglo-Saxon areas of the British Isles, and, while many of them may date from the medieval period and even later, sufficient numbers are found in context to allow of a dating from the seventh century onwards in the Isle of Man.

It should be remarked that stones with scratched patterns, many of which might rightly be described as doodles, have rarely been recorded outside archaeological excavations in western Britain and Ireland. The Isle of Man, particularly at Cronk yn How, does, however, provide examples of such casually and incompetently drawn scribbles, but none are so varied, sophisticated and well-recorded as those found within the last twenty years at St Marnock's Chapel on Inchmarnock, Bute, where the twelfth- or thirteenth-century chapel is surrounded by burials dating from the late sixth century to the Reformation.

The Maughold community

The groups of sculpture from Maughold discussed in this chapter, as well as other stones from the site, including the various inscribed crosses, help in the interpretation of the physical character of the monastic community in which they were erected. The original site has continued in use as a

Christian cemetery from the beginning of the sixth century with a few
extensions until the present day. Most of the features and finds from
Maughold (including many of the sculptural fragments) have been discovered as the result of grave-digging in the last two hundred years and provide, therefore, episodic and often incoherent topographical evidence. The
four so-called keeills (fig. 7) scattered around the churchyard, together
with the well, are quite consistent with the needs of a monastic community. The well has, however, never been scientifically examined and is now
defined by a wall of relatively modern field stones. The positions of the
keeills, by their proximity to late nineteenth-century burials which line the
churchyard wall (save on the south side where the limit has been defined
by a sharp scarp – probably an early quarry), give some impression of the
size of the original monastic site, which was perhaps 15% smaller than it is
today. Part of the original wall, bank and corner of the monastic precinct
(almost touching the well and the east end of the east keeill), noted by
archaeologists in the early part of the twentieth century, has now been
mostly obliterated by a group of twentieth-century grave plots laid down on
its line, and can only be discerned with the eye of faith. Yet within this
enclosure there existed in the early medieval period a vibrant, probably fairly rich, religious community, whose members were literate, learned and
wealthy enough to employ masons who worked to a pattern apparent
throughout the north and west of the British Isles. It was a community
which appears to have had relations chiefly with religious communities in
Northumbria, Pictland and Ireland, perhaps particularly through Whithorn
and Iona, and seems to have survived in some form into the Scandinavian
period and beyond.

CHAPTER 4

The cusp of the Scandinavian settlement of the Isle of Man

PERHAPS the most difficult decisions of attribution of the Manx memorial stones concern those produced in the ninth and early tenth century, in the period before the settlement of the Island by settlers of Scandinavian origin, either directly from Scandinavia, or from Scandinavian settlements in the Scottish islands or the lands around the Irish Sea. It is in this period that the roots of the remarkable series of tenth and early eleventh-century crosses are dimly perceived.

The political structure of the British Isles in the Viking Age

The activities of Danes and Norwegians in the British Isles in the Viking Age took many forms, from piracy and raiding, to plunder, punitive taxation and political conquest. The late ninth-century settlement of much of eastern England followed military victories, and led to local political reorganisation and the intermarriage of locals and incomers; all this on the back of political expediency and a growing trading economy. Ultimately, for a few decades from the end of the tenth to the second quarter of the eleventh century, this was to lead to the appearance of Danish kings on the throne of England. Elsewhere, settlement of incomers under chieftains led to political change which lasted for many centuries, particularly in the Northern and Western Isles of Scotland and the Isle of Man, until in 1266 the Treaty of Perth effectively saw the end of Scandinavian rule in Britain (save that Orkney and Shetland survived under the control of the Norwegian Crown for some time). The Irish story is more complicated, but enormously important, as it testifies to the flourishing development of the Irish Sea economy, from trading towns established and governed by Scandinavians under sufferance of the frequently-changing Irish political set-up, until the English conquest of 1169.

The first recorded piratical attack by Scandinavians ('heathen men') on the British Isles was in 793, when the 'raiding of heathen men miserably devastated God's church in Lindisfarne with plunder and slaughter'. This was the prelude to thirty years of raiding.

Within a few years of the attack on Lindisfarne, Irish monasteries (in the absence of towns the major economic as well as religious institutions of the country) were plundered and the country harried, and slaves and portable wealth were carried off. The Irish, used to warring attacks on their rich monasteries by compatriots, rebuilt and refortified them. But the threat of the foreigners would not go away. After a period of initial raiding the Scandinavians (mainly Norwegians) realised the potential of Ireland as a source of wealth and, seeing opportunities for trade, built fortresses (*long-phuirt*) and established trading stations around the coast, some of which became towns. One such was the site of a market at Woodstown on the County Waterford bank of the River Suir, which they developed and defended with an embankment in the middle years of the ninth century – the predecessor of the major town of Waterford. Their most important foundation, however, was along the River Liffey, on a site that became Dublin. From such places the incomers began to control the north/south trade through the Irish Sea, from the rich waters of the North Atlantic to the west coast of France, aided and sometimes challenged by a growing Norwegian polity in the Northern and Western Isles of Scotland. All the time harried by various warring 'kingdoms' of Ireland, in 902 they withdrew for a short period and invaded North Wales and the eastern shore of the Irish Sea into Dumfries and Galloway. Until this time they seem to have left the Isle of Man relatively undisturbed.

In England seasonal raiding had continued sporadically from the end of the eighth century, becoming more serious as groups of Scandinavians wintered in temporary encampments and lived on the surrounding country. But their ambitions soon changed, so that in the year 876, according to the *Anglo-Saxon Chronicle*, a Viking leader, Healfdene, and his Scandinavian (chiefly Danish) followers 'shared out the land of the Northumbrians and proceeded to support themselves'. Thus was founded the Scandinavian kingdom of York. Other settlements by treaty and by forced settlement followed, so that by the end of the third quarter of the ninth century much of England east of a line drawn from the Mersey to the mouth of Thames estuary had been settled by the invaders – a boundary still indicated today by the many place-names of Scandinavian origin in what became known as the Danelaw. Infiltration from the kingdom of York across the Pennines into Cumbria towards the end of the ninth century began a process which was to be strengthened after 902 by the arrival of a substantial number of Scandinavian refugees from the west, who soon apparently controlled the areas bordering the whole mainland coastline of the Irish Sea from Anglesey to the Mull of Galloway and southern Scotland.

By this time the northern and western islands of present-day Scotland had apparently come under the control of a fairly tough lot of pagan Norwegians, who seem to have controlled the sea routes into the Irish Sea and had established a major seat of power (an earldom) in Orkney. They also seem to have created a 'kingdom' in the Western Isles of Scotland, which is first briefly mentioned in 973, when, according to the *Anglo-Saxon Chronicle* (supplemented by the twelfth-century chronicler Florence of Worcester), a 'king of many islands', 'Maccus' (presumably equivalent to the Norse 'Magnus') pledged allegiance, with seven other sub-kings (including Kenneth, 'king of the Scots', and Malcolm, 'king of the Cumbrians'), to the English king Edgar at Chester. Whether the Isle of Man was included in the territorial title 'many islands' is not certain, but it is likely that the chronicler was referring to the Western Isles of Scotland and the Isle of Man as a unit, as they demonstrably were a century later.

Scandinavian settlement in Cumbria and the Isle of Man

The earliest evidence for Scandinavian settlement in Cumbria and the Isle of Man is indicated in the pagan custom of accompanied burial, which appears in Cumbria and on the Island at more or less the same time – in Cumbria at the very end of the ninth and in the Island, slightly later, more probably at the beginning of the tenth century.

The story has only slowly been unravelled. In 1789 a mound at Aspatria in Cumbria was excavated, and published three years later. In it was a male burial, contained within a stone cist, and accompanied by weapons – a sword, spearhead and possibly a shield-boss, as well as an axe-head and the remains of a snaffle-bit and a strap-end and buckle, possibly made locally. In 1997 further excavations at the site produced a tinned buckle, a folding knife and another axe-head. A further grave was discovered below a mound in 1822 a few miles to the north, at Hesket-in-the-Forest, in which a number of other objects of Scandinavian type turned up, including the remains of a sword with a curved guard decorated with a Norwegian interlace ornament in the tenth-century Borre style (see below p.84ff), which provides a comfortable early tenth-century date for the grave. Only a few such mound-burials have been found in Cumbria; all save one are male burials – usually warriors with their weapons. The exception was found in a small sandy mound near Claughton Hall in Lancashire, just over the border from present-day Cumbria, and was accompanied by grave-goods which include a pair of oval brooches of a type commonly found in women's graves throughout Scandinavia. Male items, including a sword, spear-head and axe, found in the same mound suggest that this was a double burial of a man and a woman. Weapons found in churchyards in Cumbria and north-ern Lancashire, at West Seaton and Rampside for example, probably indi-cate Scandinavian burials (perhaps of settlers) in pre-existing Christian cemeteries, a feature also recorded in the Isle of Man.

None of these graves, and most of the small number of other graves and burial goods found in the region, were excavated by modern methods, but in 2004 the find of a small cemetery of six burials – presumably those of a pagan family – at Cumwhitton, near Carlisle, was a game-changer in that it was properly excavated. No mounds were found here (although one of the male graves may originally have been sealed by a modest mound). The gender mix of the cemetery was marked; there were two female graves, each with pairs of typically Scandinavian oval brooches, and two male graves, each with a sword, one of which also included a spear-head. The skeletons had not survived in the acid soil, so the sex of two other burials which were unaccompanied by grave-goods could not be determined. What the Cumwhitton graves seem to demonstrate is that a family of set-tlers – still pagan – had established themselves and were living a fairly nor-mal life under an authority which tolerated them. The presence of a few minor objects (belt-mounts, for example) which had been made by non-Scandinavian craftsmen suggests that life in the region had become fairly stable.

The mound-burials in Cumbria may well be those of major landowners (even land-takers) in the region. In a pre-literate society there was no writ-ten evidence of ownership of land; a major ancestral mound could provide strong evidence to support an heir's claim to land. Although there is some evidence that women could inherit land in the Viking Age, most landown-ers were men; it is thus hardly surprising that few female mound-burials have been found in Norway or in western Scandinavian settlements in Cumbria, the Western Isles and the Isle of Man (see below). The fragility of many of the objects found in female flat graves, compared to such substantial objects of male equipment as swords and stirrups, may account for elements of this lacuna (although at Cumwhitton substantial oval brooches provide undisputed evidence of both the date, sex and status of two buried persons, who were clearly of Norwegian origin).

The pagan graves in Cumbria, while in many ways reflecting a similar pattern to that of the Isle of Man, are subtly different, partly because of evolving excavation techniques, but also because of the different nature of the female graves. In the Island a similar number of mound-burials have been excavated, some scientifically in the 1940s. The Manx mound-burials, however, represent warriors only, one even including a female who was almost certainly a sacrifice, a rite pointing to a significant pagan Scandinavian presence in the Island in the early tenth century. No female mound-burials have yet been found; indeed, women's graves with grave-goods only occur at two sites (the details of the find circumstances of one of which are now lost) and are of completely different character to those found at Cumwhitton. The most richly-furnished female burial in the Isle of Man, from St Patrick's Isle, contains no oval brooches (which would have been almost certain proof of her Norwegian origin), nor indeed any object, save a roasting spit, which could have been made in Scandinavia. This is one of a small number of other accompanied burials of both sexes excavated on St Patrick's Isle; the others are much more sparsely furnished. These burials were mostly lintel graves in a cemetery of similar burials, which otherwise had no significant grave-goods, and were presumably Christian, dating both from before and after the advent of the settlers. The graves of the earliest settlers, whether pagan or Christian, would have been dug and prepared by native Manxmen (presumably in a condition of slavery) who would have constructed traditional local lintel graves. The furnishing of the graves would, however, have been carried out by the family of the dead person according to their own religious practice or that of the deceased. As the settlement became more established, in both Cumbria and the Isle of Man, accompanied burial ceased and the practice of raising carved stone memorials over the dead would have been introduced.

Apart from offensive weapons (swords and spears), objects found in the male graves in the Isle of Man – horse-harness, ring-headed pins, shields, for example – did not generally come from Scandinavia, but from already settled lands in the Western Isles and in the Irish Sea region. More exotic finds (stirrups, strap-mounts, etc.) had their origin in France and England. The grave-goods span dates around the turn of the ninth century, and probably indicate settlement by Scandinavians who had fled from Ireland or had come secondarily from the new settlements in north-western England.

Although the evidence is slight, it would imply that the women buried in pagan graves in the Isle of Man, unlike those found in Cumbria, were not settlers who had come directly from Norway, but rather had followed their men by way of Ireland, Cumbria or western Scotland in the disturbances which affected these regions as the Scandinavians left Dublin in 902. Some of these women may even have been locals buried by men brought up in a pagan tradition. The story of Scandinavian attempts to settle in North Wales (including Anglesey), the Wirral, Cumbria (including Galloway which had already been absorbed into Northumbria) or southern Pictland, may be reasonably reconstructed from fragmentary records in the Irish annals and the Scottish Chronicle, which remain largely silent after 903 until 914, when the expelled Scandinavian settlers began to re-take their Irish possessions. (Although there is some evidence of raiding and other activity by the Dublin exiles in northern Ireland in the intervening years.) Historians have assumed that the Isle of Man would have been included in the destinations of the expelled Dublin Scandinavians at the same time, and this is quite likely, but whether there were any Scandinavian settlers in the Island before 902 is a moot point.

Increasingly important evidence of the Scandinavian presence in Cumbria, resulting from the activities of metal detectorists, is provided by the large number of hoards of silver found in north-west England. In most parts of the Viking world at this time the economy was not based on a stan-dardised coinage (as it was in the Anglo-Saxon kingdoms and the Carolingian Empire), but on precious metal by weight. Thus the hoards found in this region contained, as well as silver coins minted in different centres (some as far away as Baghdad), ingots roughly cast of silver waste and precious objects, some whole, but often cut into pieces – 'hack-silver' – and treated as bullion. Many of these hoards were buried deliberately, presumably by local landowners for safe keeping at a time of turmoil, in the early part of the tenth century when Scandinavians from their kingdom of York, Mercia, Scotland and Ireland were stirring the pot in the north-west. Many hoards were impressively large. Some were probably stolen booty, hidden by members of marauding bands of warriors, who never returned to retrieve their potential wealth. The largest silver hoard found in the British Isles, among the largest known from the whole of the Scandinavian-influenced world, was found at Cuerdale on the banks of the River Ribble, its deposit dated to *c.*905-910. It weighed about 42.2 kilograms and comprised 7,500 coins and more than 1,000 pieces of hack-silver and ingots. Nobody has convincingly interpreted the reason for its deposit, but, being hidden shortly after the arrival in the area of the Dublin Scandinavians, it might well have been buried by a group of these refugees or be the war-chest of the leader of a major raiding band, possibly from York, taking advantage of them. In the Isle of Man, to the contrary, the earliest properly-recorded hoards do not date earlier than the middle of the tenth century. Intriguingly, recent finds from metalworking sites have produced a hint of a similar, but different and earlier, mix. Among other fragments of waste silver were five silver coins of the second quarter of the ninth century from the Arab caliphates, cut into quarters by traders. These might hint at less threatening conditions, when there would have been trading contact with English or Scandinavian traders and with Anglo-Saxon silver coins before any major Scandinavian settlement.

The permanent presence of Scandinavians in north-west England in the tenth century is emphasised not only by the character of the grave-goods, but also by a number of place-names constructed with Scandinavian elements. These stress settlement by Norse speakers – names not necessarily given immediately, but gradually introduced over a period of time. Some names contain a Scandinavian personal name (e.g. *Ormr*), supplemented, for example, by an element descriptive of the type of settlement (as *-by*, meaning a farm or settlement of any size) – thus, for example, Ormesby. It has been suggested that the indigenous population was sparsely scattered in some parts of the north-west, and that the incomers had little initial social contact with the locals, who tended to retain place-names in their own language. In the Isle of Man, however, only two or three pre-Norse place-names are known (Douglas and Braddan, for example). Most Manx place-names of Celtic structure seem to have been given after the collapse of Norse power in the thirteenth century. Although place-names given by the first Scandinavian settlers and their descendants survive in the Island, they are not common, far fewer than in Cumbria. Some Scandinavian place-names may well have been introduced in the fifteenth century, when the Lancashire-based Stanley family became Kings of Man and settled a new tenantry from north-west England in the Island, settlers who introduced habitative place-names from their homeland, some of which reflected the Scandinavian settlement of the North-West.

Evidence for the size and character of the Scandinavian settlement in Man in the years immediately after 902 is exiguous. It is not impossible that some refugees from Ireland had come directly to the Island immediately after their expulsion from Dublin; but, if so, evidence would probably suggest that they would not have been numerous, and it is likely that they would have been quickly absorbed into the native population. They would have buried their dead, as did the settlers who came a few years later after 917 and the return of the exiled Scandinavians to Dublin and their other settlements in Ireland, in pre-existing native cemeteries. An important clue to what might have been a relatively easy process of settlement in these early years is provided by the apparent continuity of the religious community at Maughold, or at least the continuity of the burial ground, which was used for pagan burial before the Scandinavians adopted Christianity (the remains of at least two, and possibly three, swords of Scandinavian type were found by nineteenth-century gravediggers).

Purely pagan burials in unconsecrated ground elsewhere on the Island in the initial period of settlement is evidenced by a handful of excavated graves, including three or four male burials in mounds as was the fashion in pagan Norway. It has been suggested that burial with pagan rites in such mounds or in some other kind of prominent position on pre-existing Christian burial sites (particularly at Balladoole) was a deliberate 'violent rejection' of Christianity and a signal of a new regime. This idea has not, however, been greeted with great enthusiasm, particularly as the careful excavation of the cemetery on St Patrick's Isle clearly shows continuity of use from the pre-Scandinavian period of Christianity, through the Scandinavian period, into the Middle Ages and beyond. Continuity is also supported by the use of both Christian and pagan images on the stone memorial crosses raised soon after the Scandinavian settlement, presumably sanctioned by Christian clerics who had, perhaps in reduced circumstances, survived the land-taking. Even though the theory of violent rejection has been accepted by few students, there can be little doubt that the placing of some of the mound-burials of non-Christian character in prominent positions was simply a signal of the importance of the dead man, and possibly an aggressive symbol of the takeover of the land and the establishment of a landed family.

As will be shown, there are remarkable examples of a tolerant syncretism of pagan and Christian in the iconography of the tenth-century crosses, a feature also seen in north-west England and Yorkshire. Further, inscrip-

tions on the Manx stones suggest intermarriage between the incoming people and at least some of the indigenous inhabitants of the Island (below
pp.132-5), while the stones themselves show a relatively relaxed interpretation of Christianity by the incomers who, if not already Christian, gradually converted. All this might suggest that the Norse takeover of the Isle
of Man was a gradual process, and that integration of Scandinavian and
native was, although probably brutal in its early stages, not totally uncom-
fortable for native landowners and for any slaves taken or made as the new
order settled in. Labour and advice about local conditions and resources
would have been needed by the settlers to work the land and survive eco-
nomically, and most of the native population would have been so
employed, probably under varying conditions of servitude. There is some
evidence of intermarriage between the two groups of settlers, but the evidence is complicated by lack of linguistic definition of personal names (see
chapter 6). It is at least likely that the male settlers might not always have
brought their own women with them, and would have soon taken up with
local women.

If we take a random date ten years after the Scandinavian return to
Dublin, it is likely that the political situation on the Irish Sea littoral would
have settled down as a strong English king consolidated his power in
Northumbria and in Lancashire and Cheshire. By this time the Island
would have accepted Scandinavian authority. Unfortunately, however, we
have little or no evidence of the actual political structure of the region, save
for the existence of small 'kingdoms'. It would seem sensible to suppose
that the re-conquest of Dublin would have drawn Scandinavians back from
north-west England and while some of the latter may have remained after
the resettlement, many would have returned to their workshops, farms and
families after the campaign had been satisfactorily concluded. A few would
have settled in the Isle of Man.

It seems possible that by 927 the English king had control of the North-
West to the River Ribble and beyond, while Cumbria was settled partly
through purchase by wealthy Scandinavians, who, as Griffiths has suggested, 'had no alternative but to bow to local conditions', and who after the
middle of the century had, '...built extensive familial connections amongst
the existing population'. There was certainly a lot of silver floating around
in north-west England at this time, as is shown by the fifteen or so rich silver hoards belonging to the period after the expulsion of the Scandinavians
from Dublin; so purchase of land with this money was feasible, particular-

ly as the population in the region – both English and Scandinavian – was thinly and widely dispersed. That the purchase of land was acceptable, and that money was available for such purposes, at least on a grand scale, is indicated by the well-known grant of land by the English King Athelstan of the vast territory, north of the Ribble as far as Cockermouth, to the Church of York in June 934, which the king records had been 'bought with no little money of my own'. The grant (although a corrupt document, it probably has an authentic base and reflects contemporary practice) was issued at Nottingham, newly released from Scandinavian control. Among the vast array of bishops and nobility who witnessed it were six 'earls' with Scandinavian names, who may well even have been the financial beneficiaries of the royal transaction.

It is against this background, based on the exiguous surviving evidence from many sources, that we may postulate that the Isle of Man was settled by Scandinavians gradually easing their way in and taking possession of land by enslavement or plain robbery, or by taking over farms by marrying into local families – presumably sometimes, but not necessarily always, under duress – and even purchase. By the middle of the tenth century rich hoards began to appear in the Island; so rich are the Manx hoards that Mark Blackburn has described the Island as, 'the most intensively hoarded area of the British Isles, and even in Scandinavia its density of finds is exceeded only by the [Baltic] islands of Gotland, Öland and Bornholm'. The hoards (which were laid down between *c*.950 and *c*.1070) indicate not only the prosperity of the newcomers as farmers or traders, but also their success as warriors. As their kinsmen consolidated their political and economic power elsewhere in the region from bases in Ireland and the Scottish Isles, they drew on the mercenary element in the Manx Scandinavian population to share rich pickings through adventure, particularly between 917 and 1014 when there were at least twenty-five skirmishes and battles between the Dublin Scandinavians and the native Irish armies. Having no land boundaries with neighbouring kingdoms, the toughs of the Isle of Man were recruited, presumably with silver, for documented adventures in Wales and in the kingdoms of the north as far as Norway. But the Island was also attacked from time to time, and the prudent clearly hoarded their wealth. Whereas Cumbria and the North-West gradually became English, the Isle of Man was involved on one side or the other with the Norse kings of Dublin and Norway, and retained a varying autonomy as they built up their own Norse kingdom of Man and the Isles, a polity which was to last in one form or another until 1266.

The Norse settlement of the Isle of Man, as suggested above, if initially probably bloody, was probably not achieved by mass invasion. The suppressed non-landed native population spoke a form of Gaelic, presumably Brythonic as spoken in Galloway, Cumbria and North Wales. However, traces of the language only survive in the place-names, although only two or three pre-Norse place-names survive. It is likely that place-names containing Scandinavian elements were, as in Cumbria, only gradually introduced, as the incomers took over the Island and became dominant. The first document in Manx vernacular was, however, not written down until the sixteenth century.

The seeming respect shown by the Norse settlers for the Christian cemeteries of the indigenous inhabitants has been suggested above, while, as will be shown, the incomers' custom of raising carved stone memorials over the dead, following the fashion of the native inhabitants, indicates their early conversion to Christianity. Their conversion is demonstrated by a careful reading of inscriptions in the Old Norse language, carved in Norwegian runes on tenth-century memorial crosses, and emphasised by the evidence recorded on stones of intermarriage between native and incomer (below, chapter 6).

Sculpture on the Island – the beginning of decoration

Few decorated stone memorial monuments of the early tenth century are known in Norway or Sweden (a few of the many stones in Denmark may be roughly contemporary, while exceptions on the Baltic island of Gotland, to the far east of Sweden, need not concern us here). Traces of wooden posts above pagan mound-burials have occasionally been revealed by careful excavation in Scandinavia and in some of their colonies, the only Manx example being that at Ballateare, Jurby. Such wooden posts could have had (runic) inscriptions and other decoration, but this, while likely, is yet to be proven. It is probable, therefore, that some of the settlers encountered the practice of raising Christian memorial stones for the first time on their arrival in the Island. But many could have seen them elsewhere. In the late ninth century Scandinavian settlers in England, having encountered elaborately-carved stone memorial crosses in the Anglo-Saxon tradition, adopted them to their own taste as they converted to Christianity. On the west coast of Scotland they would have seen the grand carved crosses at important sites like Iona, as well as a host of more modest undecorated crosses of the type found in the Isle of Man, including a few decorated crosses influenced from Pictland. The simpler Welsh or Irish memorial stones and the grand High Crosses of Ireland, however, seem to have had little influence on the Scandinavian land-takers of the Isle of Man.

In Cumbria Scandinavian settlers from either Norway or Ireland had, on conversion, adopted the idea of memorial sculpture. Initially these stones were based mainly on the memorial standing crosses from across the Pennines in the Scandinavian kingdom of York, where the settlers had developed their own decorative style, combining Scandinavian motifs with Northumbrian decoration, which had been developed in the kingdom before Healfdene's land-taking in 876.

The stones of the Isle of Man in the period after the conversion of the sixth/seventh century were, as has been shown, relatively plain. Some, probably to be dated to the sixth century, were inscribed and have no further embellishment (see above, Chapter 2). Others are undatable, bearing simple, sharply-incised crosses with no elaboration, save occasionally with an incised ring crossing the arms and shaft. Some stones are embellished with crosses of different shapes outlined in a single line, often crudely, even amateurishly, executed; many, however, are carved with care and an understanding of the material. A number of simple linear crosses with wedge-shaped terminals are more meaningful; for example the three incidental crosses in one corner of the panel of a corner-post shrine from Ronaldsway, Malew (164; fig. 15), presumably represent the crucifixion of Christ and the two thieves on Calvary, and are apparently subservient to the compass-drawn encircled cross which dominates the middle of the stone. Meaningful in a different sense are the two secondary crosses on the inscribed stone Maughold 47 (fig. 13 and p.31), where the heads of the cross are extended by a hook on the right to form the *chi-rho* monogram, for the name of Christ, which may be dated to the seventh/eighth century.

While the memorial crosses mentioned above can be dated well before the Scandinavian settlement of the Island, or can chronologically be ignored as undatable, two groups of stones, mostly from Maughold, recognised and discussed in the previous chapter, may also be dated to the pre-Scandinavian period and probably to the eighth/ninth century. Both groups have plain unadorned crosses, carefully incised in panels on mudstone (e.g. no. 51; fig. 17), or carved in low relief on sizable granite slabs with slightly curved tops (e.g. no. 90).

Form and embellishment

By the time the Scandinavians had arrived in the Isle of Man and been converted, there had been a certain amount of standardisation in the form of the memorial stones, which had long left behind the rather casual placing of circles enclosing crosses made up of compass-drawn chords (as on Maughold 46) or slabs with carefully outlined crosses set within a rectangular incised frame (e.g. fig. 17). On the cusp of the newcomers' arrival, the Island's sculptors still carved the form of the whole cross in outline or low relief on a single face of a stone only. But the contour of the cross-head was beginning to extend beyond the sides of a simple rectangular slab, whether it had a rounded top (as on Lonan 71; fig. 22) or not. Another cross from Lonan (73; fig. 25 left), with its large circular head extending well beyond the sides of a squat shaft, and its blanket of interlace filling both the cross-head and its ring on one face of the stone, had possible prototypes in Maughold 70 and Lonan 71 (fig. 22). These crosses had clearly developed from the simple tall slab, often tapering towards the foot, but they now allowed the mason to cut a broad circle for the whole cross-head, and provided panels on either side of a relief-carved shaft on the otherwise plain face of the stone (as on Lonan 71).

A number of attempts have been made to erect a detailed typology of stone sculpture of the eighth to eleventh centuries in the British Isles. But, while useful in terms of accurate description, such a typology is of little chronological value in the Isle of Man. Suffice it to say that the incoming Scandinavians, arriving directly from their countries of origin, where they had no such monuments, and being totally unfamiliar with Christian iconography and symbolism before the early tenth century, simply adopted the form and shape which they found in their new country. Such was the case with the Scandinavian settlers of northern England. Only in the treatment of the surfaces of the monuments did they develop their own decorative and ornamental ideas and motifs. As in other regions, they were constrained by the geology of the material available; thus the forms they used tended to be similar to those used by their predecessors.

The situation was initially rather different in western Britain. Plain hemispherical bosses on otherwise undecorated cross-slabs of the pre-Scandinavian period in the Isle of Man (e.g. Maughold 68; fig. 20) are derived from the similar – but often highly embellished – bosses found on free-standing crosses of similar date from the Western Isles of Scotland (most notably from Iona), from Pictland and on the early High Crosses of

Fig. 24. Onchan 85. An elaborate form of bossed cross. Decorated on both faces; that illustrated is presumably the front face, as the back is less deeply carved and lacks the bosses. Height: 149cm.

Ireland, as well as on elaborately-decorated metalwork from Pictland and Ireland. The use of such bosses carries over onto free-standing decorated crosses like Lezayre 83 and (more elaborately) Onchan 85 (fig. 24), both of which are decorated on two faces and must be dated to the end of the ninth or beginning of the tenth century, the cusp of the Scandinavian period. Maughold 68 (fig. 20), a plain full-length cross in relief with a single boss in the middle of the cross-head, is unique in that it is carved on both faces of the stone. It clearly belongs to the pre-Scandinavian series and may merely be a one-off, foreshadowing the two-face decoration which was beginning to creep in at the end of the ninth century.

Manx ornament of the early tenth century and its origins

Crucial to an understanding of the sculptured stones of the Scandinavian period in the Isle of Man is the status of the monastic community at Maughold. While it may have suffered at the hands of the incoming settlers, it is more likely that any pillaging or destruction of the foundation would, however traumatic, have been a brief episode in casual raids on the

Island by piratical elements of roving Vikings. We know nothing of the wealth of the monastery at this period – but portable wealth would be subject to the law of diminishing returns and, after any raid, if the manpower was not seriously diminished by enslavement, rebuilding, clearly documented in Ireland, would almost immediately have been initiated and the religious life resumed, albeit in impoverished form. Such was certainly the case at the great Irish monasteries, such as Clonmacnoise and Armagh, and at the Irish foundation at Iona, and, almost certainly, at Whithorn. The Irish monastic centres, wealthy and prestigious, were subjects of attack not only by Scandinavians, but more frequently in the course of the continuous internecine struggle for power by factions within the various Irish kingdoms. It was for this reason that they were fortified by enclosing walls, and ultimately by strongly-built round towers which would have served as effective, if temporary, refuges for people and treasure (an example of which is to be seen on St Patrick's Isle off the west coast of the Isle of Man). At Clonmacnoise, for example, a great earthen bank enclosed the main area of activity, some 125ha in extent, as defence (clearly not always successful!) against some eight Scandinavian and twenty-seven attacks by other ambitious Irish elements between 832 and 1163. Before the foundation of Dublin and the other towns founded by the Scandinavians, monasteries were in effect the only large communities to fortify themselves from attacks by all factions. What is more, such monasteries were the only native centres of real non-local economic activity and therefore accumulated wealth.

The situation on Iona was initially rather different. There is clear evidence that the majority of its establishment, with its abbot Cellach, removed to Ireland and built a monastery at Kells in Co. Meath after a series of Viking attacks between 795 and 806. But a rump remained. The monastery on Iona gradually regained its status in the course of the ninth century and, despite various vicissitudes was, as late as 980, important and secure enough to be the place of retirement, as a monk, of Olaf Cuarán, the Scandinavian king of Dublin. The monastery of Whithorn, although seemingly sacked towards the end of the ninth century, was not so open to attack as Iona; set back out of sight of the sea, its trading function at the beginning of the Viking Age was conducted through beach markets at some distance from the monastery (as at a number of other monasteries around the western coasts of Britain – most notably at St David's, inland from the Pembrokeshire coast) and seems to have received less attention from Viking raiders. Like the nearby ecclesiastical establishment of Kirkmadrine,

*Fig. 25 left. Lonan 73; height: 251cm. Right. Braddan 72; height: 132cm. The diame-
ter of the heads of both crosses is the same. Lonan still stands outside the church, but may
not be in its original position. A tenon on its foot is slotted into a large flat oval stone to
hold it in place. The basal socketed stone is probably original. Cf. the tenon in fig. 33.*

it developed in the late ninth or early tenth century an individual ornamental style for its carved stone crosses – a style in some ways linked to
those found in Dumfries and Cumbria, but in no way influenced by
Scandinavian taste.

If it is correct that the Scandinavian settlement of the Isle of Man was a
gradual process, it would seem likely, by parallel to the situation in Ireland
and Galloway, that the monastery at Maughold continued to function as a
community into the period of the Scandinavian settlement. Incoming settlers began to be buried in the cemetery there – as witness the find of two
(and possibly three) swords by gravediggers in the churchyard, and the
presence of stone crosses embellished with Scandinavian motifs and decoration on the site. It would seem that the native sculptors, long established
at Maughold, continued to work there, like their contemporaries in
Galloway, they were adventuring into a more elaborate ornamental style.

Unlike their contemporaries in Galloway, however, the Manx sculptors were soon, as will be demonstrated in the next chapter, adopting Scandinavian motifs and images.

Towards the end of the ninth century, as has been shown, a number of elaborately-decorated crosses had been produced in the Isle of Man, of which many were of high quality. The main purely decorative element in Manx stone sculpture at this period, as in the rest of the British Isles at the time, comprised various patterns of simple interlaced ribbon ornament of varied pattern and complication which filled (one might almost say plastered) many of the available surfaces of the stone (cf. fig. 25). In Ireland and Pictland interlace patterns, including vine-scrolls and contorted animal ornament, had long supplemented the trumpet-spirals of prehistoric 'Celtic' origin.

The Scandinavians who settled in England in the late ninth century were introduced to a sculptural tradition totally foreign to them. As they converted to Christianity and began to bury their dead in Christian mode, the more affluent among them began to raise memorial crosses based on those produced for the local population. They blended the indigenous ornamental elements found there with their own ornamental motifs, most splendidly on the great tenth-century cross from Gosforth in Cumbria (fig. 26), which stands some 4.4m high and is elaborately carved with figures and interlace ornament, mostly derived from Scandinavia. Mostly, however, their sculpture was not so grand, nor so superlatively and idiosyncratically worked. They drew inspiration from both English and Scandinavian sources, most successfully blended in Cumbria. Only fine spiral ornament, however, was rejected – possibly because it was difficult to carve – in favour of simple ribbon scrolls. Slightly earlier, in the Scandinavian kingdom of York, local sculptors had adopted the taste of incomers, blending their motifs with their own. They were not always successful; at Middleton in Ryedale, for example, they produced hybrids which are clearly coarse misunderstandings of Scandinavian animal ornament.

On the Manx crosses at the end of the ninth century, on the cusp of the first Scandinavian settlement, ribbon interlace and linear patterns (meander, step and zig-zag) are the chief patterns known, together with occasional simple ribbon spirals found on a few stones, as at the foot of the otherwise-unembellished cross from Lonan (71; fig. 22, see above p.46).

Springing from the foot of this cross is a pair of simple spirals, of a form which occurs on more elaborately decorated crosses, which foreshadow the

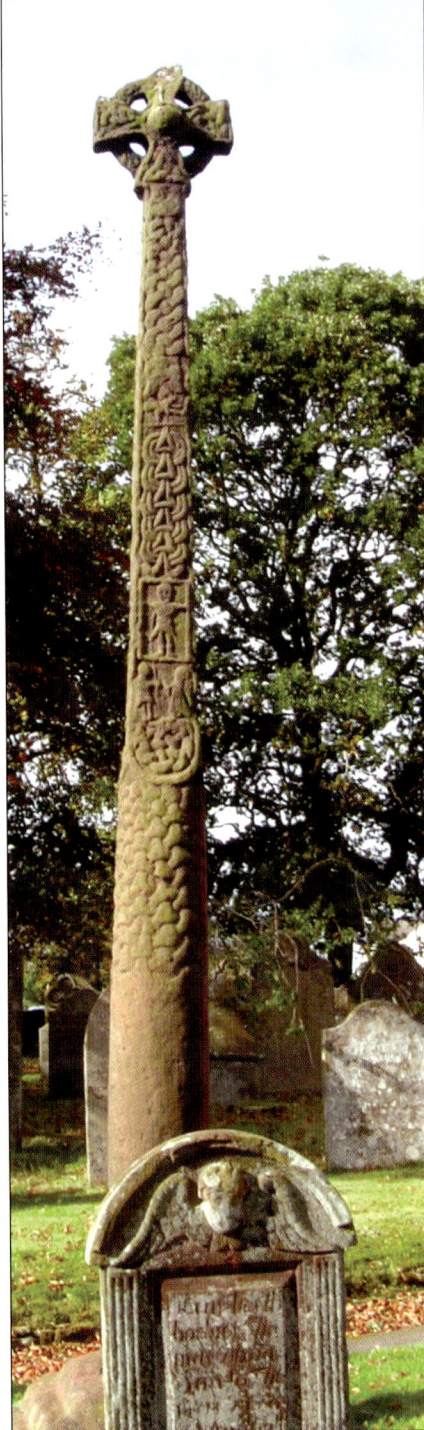

Fig. 26. Cross from Gosforth, Cumbria. Height: 442cm. Of red sandstone, this cross is contemporary with the tenth-century stones of the Isle of Man. Although it is ornamented with the Borre style ring-chain (and developments of it), it has hunting scenes as well as figures reminiscent of Scandinavian legend. In form and size it is entirely unique in the surviving corpus of early British stone sculpture.

use of this detail at the feet of a number of crosses of the Scandinavian peri-od, e.g. on Kirk Michael 132 (fig. 55, see below p.116). The single spirals at the foot of a cross presumably represent the roots of the vine or the roots of the cross, in its guise as a tree. Spirals in this position are paralleled rarely outside the Island, but do occur in Pictland and, in very derivative form, on Anglesey and on a few simple linear cross-slabs from Ireland (e.g. at Clonmacnoise, Co. Offaly). Two later crosses with this feature are known in Ireland (at Kilmainham, Dublin, and – at the base of the cross-head – at Kilfenora, Co. Clare), both of which have plain shafts and are confidently dated by Irish scholars to the late eleventh or early twelfth cen-tury. Whether the Manx examples were the first fruits of the Norse adap-tation of an indigenous monumental ornament, or a fleeting attempt to capture the tradition of the native inhabitants of the Irish Sea province, is difficult to say.

Spirals appear in various guises, chiefly filling spaces, on the pre-Scandinavian stones, as, for example, the rows of conjoined spirals on Onchan 92 (fig. 27). Double opposed spirals are seen in the side panel of Kirk Michael 194, while single spiral scrolls are used as fillers on a frag-ment from Maughold (no. 87), on Kirk Michael 94 and Bride 124. Conjoined spirals are in no way related to the 'trumpet spirals' of earlier Hiberno-Saxon (or 'Celtic') art; rather they are derived from the vine-scroll – the universal Christian 'tree of life' motif, representing Christ's saying, 'I am the true vine' (St John's Gospel, 15, 1). The vine-scroll, portrayed ver-tically, its tendrils enclosing bunches of grapes and later including animals and birds, as it appears on Northumbrian crosses, is not found in the Isle of Man, but is relatively common elsewhere in the late seventh to eighth centuries in Pictland, Ireland and Northumbria. In a more degenerate form, as a simple vegetal ornament without grapes, it occurs in the earliest period of the Scandinavian settlement in the Island in the first half of the tenth century (as on a side panel on one face of Kirk Michael 101, fig. 32; but see below p.88).

These complicated spiral patterns belong to this period of transition. Crosses were plastered with ribbon ornament, interlaced in various ways; some were closely knit, often carried out in rather irregular patterns. Most interesting is the interlace on the large wheel-headed crosses from Lonan (73; figs. 25 left and 28), Braddan (72; fig. 25 right) and Onchan (74) and on the much-damaged cross from the keeill at Cardle Veg, Maughold (86). The Lonan and Braddan crosses have heads of the same size and may well have been cut from the same template, although the layout of the ornament

Fig. 27. Onchan 92. An elaborate use of spirals.
Height: 135cm.

Fig. 28. Lonan 73. Cf. fig. 25. Demonstrating the blanketing of the cross-face with interlace.

is different. The Lonan cross, unlike the others, has ribbon ornament on the cross-head and on the elaborate ring, but not in the fields formed of the armpits. It also has four transverse lines of different interlace patterns at the top of a stumpy shaft. Three of the animals between the arms of Braddan 72 are backward-looking (the fourth is much damaged). The animal in the top-right armpit in particular is related to animals of the late ninth-century Anglo-Saxon Trewhiddle style; specifically to an animal on a nielloed silver strap-end from Whitby, where the leg of the animal crosses its body in a similar fashion. The human mask between two animals on the upper arm of the cross is copied from a motif of a man between two animals which,

questionably labelled as 'Daniel in the lion's den', is common in Western
Europe from the sixth century onwards.

Just as the early, long pre-Scandinavian, carved crosses from Maughold
were clearly influenced from the Whithorn area, so some of this Manx
group of crosses had similar inspiration. At Whithorn, and at a small number of other sites in Galloway, elaborate and regular ribbon interlace patterns, with no trace of Scandinavian influence, had become the only ornamental feature, blanketing the whole of the cross face. As at Maughold, the
carvers of crosses from that part of Galloway which lies to the east of
Kirkcudbright had retreated from the production of the simple linear
designs of the earlier period. Increasingly influenced by the Northumbrians
who now controlled the diocese, they presumably forged closer links with
the Anglian sculptural tradition dominant in Dumfries and eastern
Cumbria. Their crosses no longer had much direct influence on the interlace patterns produced in the Isle of Man, although the idea of blanket-cov-
ering surfaces with interlace is common to both eastern Galloway and the
Island. It is also seen in a rather more mechanical form on a number of
recumbent grave-covers from Govan outside Glasgow, which seem to be
successors to Pictish-influenced crosses. Their double-stranded interlace is
closely paralleled on a tightly-carved interlace on a fragment from
Maughold (108), which is closely related to patterns on crosses from
Whithorn and Monreith. In the late ninth and early tenth centuries in most
of Northumbria and Cumbria (but not in Galloway) there was, as at
Maughold, a gradual loosening of the austerity of the earlier work. This was
to lead to an adventurous use not only of ribbon interlace, but also of historiated scenes depicting hunts as well as pagan mythology and Christian
symbolism.

Three extraordinary crosses (Onchan 92 and 93 and, from Bishopscourt,
Kirk Michael 94) are clearly related by their interlace patterns to the three
stones, nos. 72-4, discussed above. The interlace is in no way out of the
ordinary, but the strange figures on either side of the cross-shaft on Onchan
92 (fig. 27), with spiral hips, elongated bodies and fierce heads are unique
to Man and seem almost to be incompetent attempts by a sculptor, used to
carving interlace, to produce an image of a monster unlike any other found
outside the Island (but see below p.73). The abundance of spiral motifs on
all three crosses is also unusual in that they are positioned in so casual a
manner. Although some spirals clearly relate to representations of the roots
of a tree, as on the cross from Lonan (71; fig. 22, above p.46), others might
refer to an origin in the vine-scroll.

Hunting scenes

Of this group Kirk Michael 94 introduces a new feature to the Island series of immediately pre-Scandinavian sculpture, in that this cross-slab is decorated on both faces and on both edges, as on most of the crosses of Scandinavian date. The edges have simple interlaced ribbon running from top to bottom. The ornament in the main field on one face is now completely worn away, but the ribbon interlace of the ring round the head is different from that on the other, better-preserved, face. Interestingly, traces of hunting scenes are to be seen at the base of the slab on either side. (These scenes are now almost completely obliterated, but are clearly delineated in Kermode's published wash-drawings, made before 1907. Unfortunately they are not so clearly seen on photographs of the same period.) The panel beside the cross on the best-preserved face depicts a strange monster which can only be explained in relation to the Onchan crosses described above (nos. 92 and 93).

A slab from Maughold (97), of which most of one side is now missing, is also decorated on both faces and its surviving edge (fig. 29) and is clearly related to the three crosses discussed above. It differs from them in that it is rather more disciplined in its ornament, and has no monstrous animal. Rather it has, below the cross-shaft, a hunting scene on one face, and an antlered deer and hound involved in a complicated hunting scene on the other. Ribbon interlace fills the stem of the crosses carved on both faces – on one face is double stranded ribbon and a single strand on the other. Springing from the corner of the base of the shaft are carefully coiled spirals. A line of running dogs, part of a hunting scene, appears below a group of four spirals in the side panel on the right-hand face of the slab (not illustrated), while in the surviving side panel on the other face a cloaked man stands, grasping the border of the cross with his hand. This figure could conceivably have deteriorated into the strange monsters in the side panels of the Onchan slabs (92, fig. 27; and 93) and the apparently seated man on Kirk Michael 94.

There is no specific trace of any Scandinavian influence on Maughold 97 (fig. 29), but the Pictish influence is clear. The scenes of riders and dogs (apparently hunting-dogs) which appear on some pieces of Manx sculpture, first noticed in much eroded condition below the figures of Paul and Antony on Maughold 96 (fig. 21; p.44), are repeated or developed on the tenth-century stones of the Manx Scandinavian series, as on Kirk Michael 132 (fig. 55) and Andreas 131 (fig. 30) and on a number of other Manx

Fig. 29. Maughold 97. Note hunting scene at the foot of the cross. Height: 162cm.

stones. Ultimately such scenes are of Roman origin, and were adapted for use on Pictish and Irish stone memorials, particularly on the remarkable corner-post sarcophagus from St Andrew's, of eighth-century date, where its Late Antique Mediterranean influences are most clearly seen alongside some of the finest expressions of eighth-century native Pictish ornament. Hunting scenes appear on many of the late Pictish slabs, and, interestingly, on the side panel of a cross on a slab from Kirriemuir, Angus, where an upright, walking man faces towards a hunting scene in the complementary panel on the other side of the cross-shaft. Such walking hooded men appear on a number of other Pictish slabs (from e.g. Golspie, Sutherland, and Eassie, Angus), and in one case they appear, with other huntsmen (riders and archers), in the midst of a hunting scene. Is it possible that the man on Kirk Michael 94 is related to these walking men?

The form of Maughold 97, and what remains of its iconography, would point to Pictland as the source of the scene on this particular Manx slab and of its contemporaries from Onchan – a source also suggested (above pp.43-5) for the scene of Paul and Antony in the desert on Maughold 96 (fig. 21), which bears a rather static hunting scene in a secondary position at the base of the slab.

The image of the hunting scene was presumably embedded in that community of Christian learning, thinking and iconography seen at the late seventh- and eighth-century monastic foundations of Ireland, Pictland, Galloway and the Western Isles of Scotland (on Iona and at Kildonan on Eigg), but not in Northumbria. The symbolism of these scenes in Christian iconography has been much discussed, but few of the interpretations put forward are entirely convincing, partly because the scenes vary so much in their structure and in the portrayal of different beasts, but also because their relationship to any biblical or exegetic sources is obscure. What is clear is that such scenes are only occasionally encountered on the near continent, for example on a couple of more or less contemporary and rather crude sarcophagi in France. Indeed, it has been pointed out that hunting scenes in the early medieval period are better represented in Scotland than elsewhere in Europe. It is, therefore, reasonable to suppose that they may have been inspired by Romano-British sculpture or metalwork which had survived the centuries and had been seen and imitated by Pictish craftsmen.

What is surprising is the appearance of hunting scenes on the later Scandinavian crosses in the Isle of Man, where they jostle Scandinavian ornament and even symbolism. To such images on this late Manx series

Fig. 30. Andreas 131. One of the tallest complete cross-slabs on the Island. On both faces of the cross is an elaborate hunting scene. Height: 193cm.

Fig. 31. The two faces of an unusually small cross, Maughold 114. One face (left) has a normal interlace pattern typical of pre-Scandinavian crosses. On the other face (right) is a carefully-constructed, lightly-incised version of the Scandinavian Borre ring-chain. Height: 53cm.

may be added a number of varied animals, sometimes with or without reference to hunting, singly or in pairs – boars, dogs, and deer are recognisable – on Santon 95, Maughold 98 and 133, Onchan 74, Andreas 131 (fig. 30), Bride 124, Kirk Michael 132, Jurby 127 and Kirk Michael 126 – all of which may be compared to animals on crosses in Northumbria, Scotland and Ireland. This excludes purely ornamental, usually interlaced, animals, as well as animals which appear in iconographic contexts, both Christian and pagan, to which we shall return.

In this chapter I have attempted to demonstrate how ornamental elements later used in the Island in the period of Scandinavian settlement had their origin in areas that were both pagan and Christian, both within and outside its shores. As we turn to the tenth century, while traces of this ornament are still found, strong undoubtedly Scandinavian motifs make their appearance, and soon dominate the art of the Manx sculptural tradition. To illustrate the clear intrusion of a Scandinavian motif on a cross which is otherwise completely typical of the ornament found on the pre-Scandinavian series, we should turn to Maughold 114 (fig. 31). This small slab has a full-length, ring-headed cross on both faces. The ends of the cross-head and the shaft of the cross are filled with tight interlace ornament, and the middle of the cross-head is plain, save for a ring and dot in the centre. On one side the ring is embellished with a sloping step pattern and on the other, much-damaged, face the rings are filled with simple interlace patterns, two of which, unusually, terminate in simple animal heads seen from above. The shaft on one face (fig. 31 left), probably the front, had a rope-like border and is filled with a tight simple blanket of interlace of a type seen on many of the pre-Scandinavian stones (see above, p.69). The border of the shaft on the other face is rolled, and the shaft is filled with an incised, carefully drawn 'ring-chain' (fig. 31 right), typical of the Scandinavian Borre style, which is discussed in the next chapter.

CHAPTER 5
The stone sculpture of the
Scandinavian settlement

The background

THE STORY of the period leading to the Scandinavian settlement of the Island has been considered in some detail in the previous chapter. Here I shall concentrate almost exclusively on the sculpture of the tenth and early eleventh century, which provides the most coherent evidence for the religious and social record of the period following the initial settlement. The settlement appears to have been a comparatively quiet affair, although the brutal side of the incomers cannot have been far from the surface. This would have been particularly true in its early stages, when the description 'land-taking' would seem to be entirely appropriate. The paucity of written records of the Island in the period has already been pointed out, but as the century runs its course, the accounts of the scribes become more important – and often more baffling.

Some of these records, the *Anglo-Saxon Chronicle* for example, provide useful clues to the Island's history, its narrative occasionally embellished by later historians. A compilation of Irish history assembled in the late fifteenth century, *The Annals of Ulster* (*Annála Uladh*), drawn from a number of annalistic accounts (mainly in the Irish language) outlines the story of medieval Ireland from the fifth century onwards. This concentrates chiefly, but not exclusively, on the warlike activities of kings in Ireland, and occasionally in the other kingdoms around the Irish Sea. Mentions of the Isle of Man in these annals and in other Irish manuscript sources provide a biased and incomplete but, if quarried cautiously, useful series of pegs on which to hang some of the more colourful events of early medieval Manx history, mostly of a warlike nature.

The same bias and sporadic nature of the evidence is true of the Scandinavian historical sagas, particularly those assembled in twelfth- and thirteenth-century sources in *Heimskringla* (the literal meaning of which is 'disc of the world') and *Orkneyinga saga* ('Saga of the people of Orkney'). Such records fill some of the gaps and often add colour. Tenth- and eleventh-century references in these and other Scandinavian sources were not written down until the thirteenth century or even later; thus caution in citing events is imperative. However, the oral memory of historical personages and events, when they can be cross-checked, is often remarkably accurate. The runic inscriptions (see below, chapter 6) which appear with some frequency on the stone crosses in the Isle of Man are helpful in building up a picture of the contemporary social and religious life of the Manx people in the tenth century.

Evidence concerning the social history and economic background of the Island when it first came under Scandinavian control depends chiefly on the archaeological record, which has been discussed in the previous chapter. This includes the physical remains of settlements, which are sparse, together with the surprisingly rich finds of treasure comprising silver coins and other objects of precious metal, and the re-use of earlier coastal fortifications for specific purposes. The increasing indications of a Manx metalworking industry, particularly of lead and even copper which may well have been mined on the Island, are all bound up with trade and the beach markets on the shores of the Irish Sea.

Burial rites are also indicative of the changing influences of both natives and settlers. The Scandinavians soon became Christian. They began to follow the burial practices of the local inhabitants by adopting existing cemeteries to their own use, and, inspired by the carved stone memorial monuments in the many graveyards, by adapting them to their own taste and practices. Thus they produced some of the most interesting memorials to their dead encountered in the whole of the Scandinavian world during the Viking Age. It is these memorials which form the subject of this chapter.

The stones carved for the Scandinavian settlers of the Island were, at their best, of a remarkably high quality. Although based initially on the ornament used on the stones of the native inhabitants, much of the ornament used on the Manx crosses is clearly derived directly – and fairly purely – from Scandinavia, and probably from Norway. It cannot be emphasised too strongly that at the time of the Scandinavian settlement of the Isle of Man, the only part of Scandinavia that had been converted to Christianity was Denmark, and that no memorial stones of the kind found in the British Isles had been raised by the newly-converted Danes. Nor is much ornamental stone sculpture of this period known from the whole of Scandinavia, save for an important corpus of little relevance to that found in the Island, which has survived on the Baltic island of Gotland. On the other hand a certain amount of high-quality wooden sculpture is known from ninth-century Norway, the influence of some of which is faintly traced in the Isle of Man.

At the end of the previous chapter one stone, Maughold 114, was singled out as it clearly demonstrates the beginning of a synthesis between the two ornamental traditions – the native and the Norse. The well-executed tight, rounded native interlace ornament on one face of this stone (fig. 31 left, see above page 77) is balanced by an accurate, but incised linear, expression of one of the main elements of the contemporary Scandinavian ornament on the other face – the Borre-style ring-chain (fig. 31 right, see below, p.84ff). The Scandinavian settler was clearly accepting the work of the native sculptors, who presumably used the ring-chain as part of a co-operative exercise in taste. It was a motif which, as will be shown, was enthusiastically used by later craftsmen.

Conversion of the Scandinavian settlers

While it is easy to claim that the carved stone monuments of the tenth century demonstrate that the Scandinavian land-takers converted to Christianity soon after they had settled in, the process of this conversion among the Manx is otherwise hard to discern or interpret. From the rite of burial with grave-goods (see above p.53ff) it must be assumed that some of the first settlers were pagan, but the character of the grave-goods (apart from weapons), which were generally not sourced from Scandinavia, emphasises the fact that many of the settlers had lived in contact with Christians around the Irish Sea for some time. This would suggest that they had at least some understanding of the religion of the indigenous population and that some of them may well have been converted before their arrival in the Island. In the Scandinavian settlements in England it would seem that Christianity was first imposed by the English king, as did Alfred in his treaty with Guthrum at Wedmore in 878. A similar story of royal intervention is told of Harald in Denmark *c.*960, who, on a granite boulder he raised in the royal centre of Jelling, recorded that he 'won the whole of Denmark for himself … and made the Danes Christian'. In Iceland in 1000, conversion to Christianity was imposed by the great landowners at an assembly of the people and thence gradually trickled down to those of lower social status. It would seem that in those parts of Britain settled by Scandinavians, the process was sometimes reversed, as the Christian population, including priests who had survived the turmoil, gradually influenced the settlers, leading them to conversion. The settlers' initial under-standing of the new god, however they had embraced him, would have been nugatory and, as was customary in the early years of the adoption of the new religion, elements of their original beliefs would have been used exegetically as they turned to Christianity. This is emphasised by the use of images from Scandinavian myth and legend carved on the stone memori-als they raised.

The settlers were basically non-literate, in that, despite their use of the runic script, they have left no contemporary account of their religion in any written source. That we know anything of their gods is entirely due to the comparatively extensive literature which survives, written down by Christians in various forms in the thirteenth century and later. The most important of these sources are the Icelandic *Heimskringla*, mentioned above, and the *Prose Edda* and the *Poetic Edda*, all of which provide tales of myth and legend based on folk memory which went back to the early Viking Age and beyond. Such accounts were based on oral traditions of gods and heroes, and it was from these traditions that the earliest writers, all Christians, recorded the names of the pagan gods (the Æsir and Vanir), among them names well-known today: Odin, Thor, Frey and Freyja, for example. They also recounted the legend of Ragnarǫk – the destruction of the gods and the emergence of a new order – which they were to use as a parallel to the death of Christ and his resurrection. That the early Scandi-navian converts understood such syncretic interpretations, is demonstrated with regard to the Resurrection and Ragnarǫk on the surviving fragment of the cross Andreas 128 (fig. 49; see below p.106ff).

As medieval scribes over the years recalled many popular myths of the Scandinavian homelands, distinctions between myth and religion became blurred. As with most great myth cycles, the story was embroidered and extended; many Scandinavian heroes became gods and the resultant nar-rative was mixed with other traditions. Scholars of the Renaissance and the Enlightenment sought an origin for the gods and heroes elsewhere, partic-ularly in Asia. The 'neo-pagans' of today claim many of these figures for their own pantheon, be they practitioners of Ásaturú (sometimes called Odinism), followers of Frey, Goths, wiccans, neo-Nazis, Stonehenge 'druids' or whatever, and do no better than past scholars to explain the roots of their invented religion.

Both the pagan religion and the associated myths became familiar to the people who converted the Scandinavian settlers in the Isle of Man, and, by

Christian tradition handed down from the sixth-century Pope Gregory the Great to the leader of the mission to England, missionary priests would have been told to respect them and used them to illustrate their homilies. They would explain the myths in Christian terms in relation not only to the Bible, but also to such fundamental notions as the creation of the world, death, fate and the human condition. Thus there survives in the Isle of Man a group of memorial stones dominated by the Christian cross on which are carved – as visual aids to exegesis – scenes taken from the myths and religion of the pagan settlers and interpreted in Christian terms. Such illustrative material – which is clearly incomplete – can only be treated with caution today; but, despite all scepticism, we may dimly discern the threads of an earlier religion, one which can only be recounted against the background of a huge critical apparatus, in which scholars suggest how they would have been presented by monotheistic Christian priests.

The Manx crosses follow the model of the developed slab-crosses of the pre-Scandinavian period (see p.63ff), but were now consistently decorated on both faces of the stone. As on some pre-Scandinavian crosses, the heads were gradually extended outside the confines of the slab, and, as on Braddan 135, developed even further to become a free-standing, often rather elegant, tall cross, not unlike those that were being produced at the same time in Cumbria and the Scandinavian kingdom of York, a region which may have influenced the Manx sculptors of the late tenth century. The form of these Anglo-Scandinavian grave-markers had grown out of the series of grand historiated preaching-crosses of seventh- and eighth-century Christian Northumbria, of which the last surviving representative is the unique 4.4m-tall tenth-century cross from Gosforth in Cumbria (fig. 26), with its developed versions of Scandinavian ornament and complicated imagery.

Dating the stones

The chronological sequence of the Manx cross-slabs of the period of Scandinavian settlement is mainly derived from the sequence of ornamental styles in use in Scandinavia in the period when the crosses were carved in the Island. The dating of the styles is based largely on decorated wooden objects in the homelands, the chronology of which provides a reasonably accurate sequence of dates constructed on the basis of dendrochronology (i.e. tree-ring dating), which is usually accurate to within a year or two. Such dates are supplemented by metal objects decorated in the defined

styles found in coin-hoards throughout the Viking world. These coins provide the regnal dates of the kings who controlled their minting, often
refined by the re-minting of coins, thus giving reasonably accurate dates for
the deposition of the hoards and thus providing a *terminus ante quem* for the
making of objects in a hoard. A few inscribed and ornamented stones
which record the names of historical personages or political events – most
importantly the great stone raised by Harald Bluetooth (who died *c.*987) at
Jelling, Denmark – further help to support the dates of ornamental styles of
the period. Objects found in reliably recorded archaeological excavations
are also sometimes of use in providing approximate dates, particularly by
the presence in the graves of wood which can be used for dendrochrono-
logical determination. The names of the styles are taken from Scandinavian
sites in which classic examples have been found. The styles which have
been recognised in the Isle of Man, with their generally accepted dates in
their Scandinavian homelands, are listed and discussed below:

> *Borre c.850-950*
>
> *Jellinge c.900-975*
>
> *Mammen c.960-1000/25*
>
> *Ringerike c.1000-1075*

The final style of the Viking Age, the Urnes style (*c.*1050-1125), does not
occur on any of the Manx crosses.

These dates overlap – one style did not end in a particular year, to be
replaced by another. Further, two styles can appear in various forms and
modifications on the same object. The Mammen style, for example, can
sometimes only be distinguished by small differences from the Jellinge
style. All these dates are approximations, and can only be applied to the
Island with due reservation. If, however, one takes into account the political probability that the Scandinavian incomers began to make an impact on
the Island in the first quarter of the tenth century, a sliding scale of dates
can be constructed and will be used here.

The Borre style

The Borre style was extremely popular in the Island. The only motif of
the style used in the Isle of Man is an interlace ornament which appears in
two forms, as a ring-chain and as a knot (variations of the latter – sometimes called a 'pretzel' – appear on some cross-heads and continued to be
used on some of the latest monuments of the Manx series). The two forms

Fig. 32. Kirk Michael 101. The runic inscription on one edge, which spills over onto one face, records that it was carved by a man called Gautr, who claimed to have carved it 'and all in Man'. Height: 183cm.

of Borre-style ring-chain are seen in classic mode on Kirk Michael 101 (fig. 32) The basic 'trick' of the construction is a chain formed of rings with extensions at top or bottom which interlace with each other to form the 'chain' (as on the shaft of this cross). The motif is often varied; sometimes the free ring is more clearly displayed, as with the elongated interlaced ribbon on the lateral panel on this cross. Sometimes it is given a double contour (Kirk Michael 126), while in other, probably later, instances the ring is almond-shaped (Jurby 119) or beaded for emphasis as on Ballaugh 106 (fig. 33).

The Borre style, which in its homeland is much richer and more varied in motif than the simple designs which occur in the Island, may well have

Fig. 33. Ballaugh 106. The cross is here seen, c.1900, before it was cemented into the floor of the church. The tenon presumably originally fixed it in a stone base when it was erected in the churchyard (cf. fig. 25). One face has a long runic inscription in a panel on one side of the shaft; on a side panel on the other face is a classic Borre-style ring-chain. Height: 137cm.

had its origin in Norway and it must have been the Norwegian taste of the settlers which influenced its use in the Island. The ring-chain was probably first developed on such objects as copper-alloy belt- or harness-mounts like those found in a ship-burial at Borre in Vestfold, Norway (from which the style takes its name), but it is ubiquitous elsewhere in Scandinavia. A good Scandinavian parallel to the Manx motif occurs on a strap-end from Sandvor in Rogaland (fig. 34). The Manx version of this element is probably derived directly from Norway and not, as I previously thought, by way of Cumbria, where it occurs on a number of crosses. In Cumbria one element, the ring-chain, appears in classic form on the Muncaster cross and, more elaborately developed, on the great Gosforth cross (fig. 26) The ornament of the Muncaster cross differs in only minor ways from the Manx version of the Borre ring-chain, and was also clearly developed directly from a metalwork prototype. In the Isle of Man Norwegian influence is emphasised by the Old Norse name of the carver, Gautr, inscribed in runic characters on a cross-slab from Kirk Michael (101; fig. 32, see below, p.130).

It is important to note that many of the earlier complete crosses or fragments decorated with the simple Borre-style ring-chain are relatively restrained in their ornamental repertoire. Borre interlace in these cases is confined in a developed form to construct ribbon interlace on the cross-head. It is most dominantly seen in relatively strict forms of the ring-chain motif which on the shafts of the crosses, where it is often set in parallel to various linear ribbon-interlace or meander patterns in panels between the cross shaft and the edge of the slab (as on Kirk Michael 101;

Fig. 34. Copper-alloy strap-end from Sandvor, Rogaland, Norway. Classic version of the Borre style of the form found in the Isle of Man.

fig. 32). One of the linear motifs on Kirk Michael 101, and on a number of other crosses, is hard to parallel outside the Isle of Man (it occurs, however, at Lowther in Cumbria and at two other sites in West Yorkshire). It consists of a tendril which springs from alternating sides of an undulating stem to re-cross the stem and terminate in a scroll – a motif probably based on a version of the ubiquitous vine-scroll (see above p.69). The lay-out of many of these crosses in long linear panels parallel with the cross-shaft is similar in design, but not in motif, to those found on the contemporary Whithorn crosses (above p.64). In some cases, as on Jurby 125 and the much-damaged Kirk Michael 126, animals and human figures occur together in panels, while the shaft of a cross is filled with the ring-chain. On Kirk Michael 126, on a side panel of the cross-shaft, is a man who might be a bishop as he carries a tau-headed staff or crozier (a figure which occurs elsewhere on the crosses); below him (fig. 35) is a helmeted warrior holding a drawn sword pointing upwards (he is actually portrayed upside-down). In many cases, however, the shaft of the cross and the lateral panels are filled with common ribbon interlace like that which appeared on the crosses discussed in the previous chapter.

Fig. 35. Kirk Michael 126 (detail). Armed warrior. The figure (portrayed upside down) was carved on the side panel of the cross-shaft of this much-damaged stone.

Semi-naturalistic animals which are to be seen in the various hunting and other scenes have been noted in the pre-Scandinavian sculpture of the Island (e.g. on Maughold 96; fig. 21) and discussed in the previous chapter. On crosses of the Scandinavian period hunting scenes or single animals and figures, some drawn from Norse mythology, mix happily with developed ribbon knots and Christian symbols to add potential exegetical narrative to the interlace patterns on the crosses. A potential which may be imagined, for example, on a cross fragment from Jurby (125) and on one face of the great slab from Andreas (131; fig. 30, above p.76), with its undecorated cross-head.

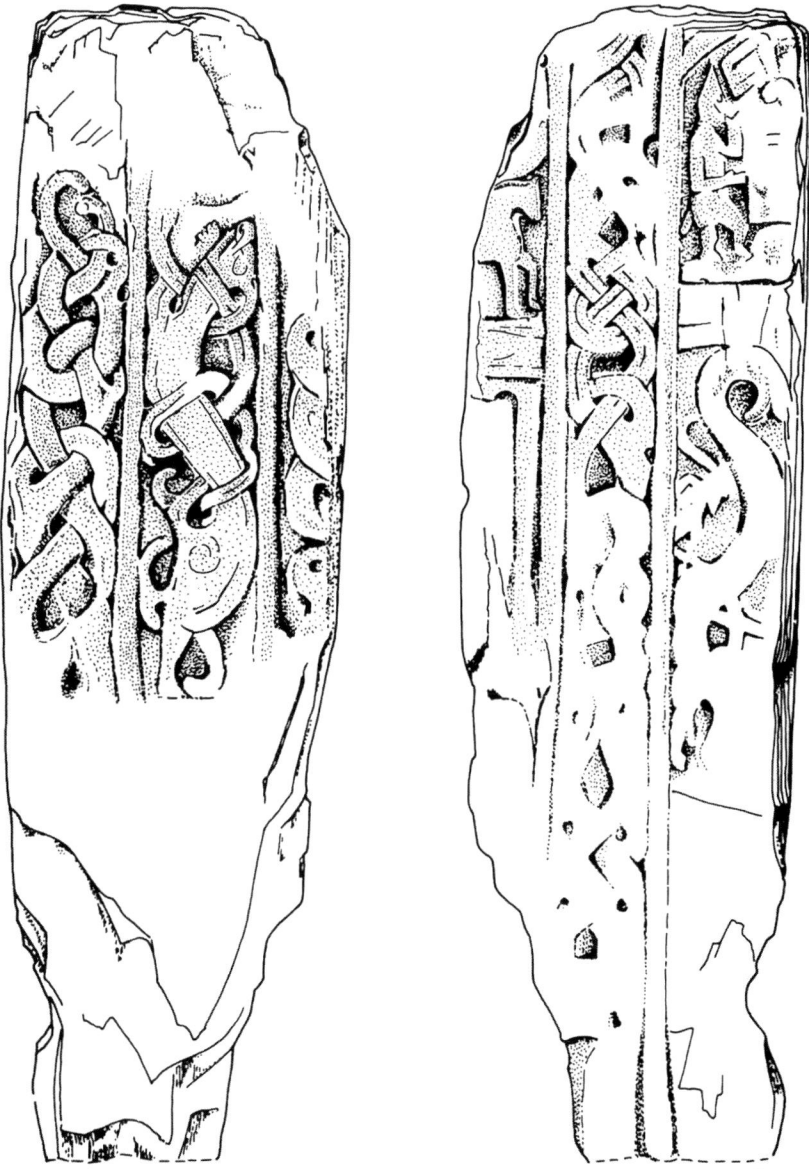

Fig. 36. Malew 120. The animal on the shaft of the cross (left) is a classic Jellinge-style creature. On the other face are scenes from the Sigurd saga. Height: 152cm.

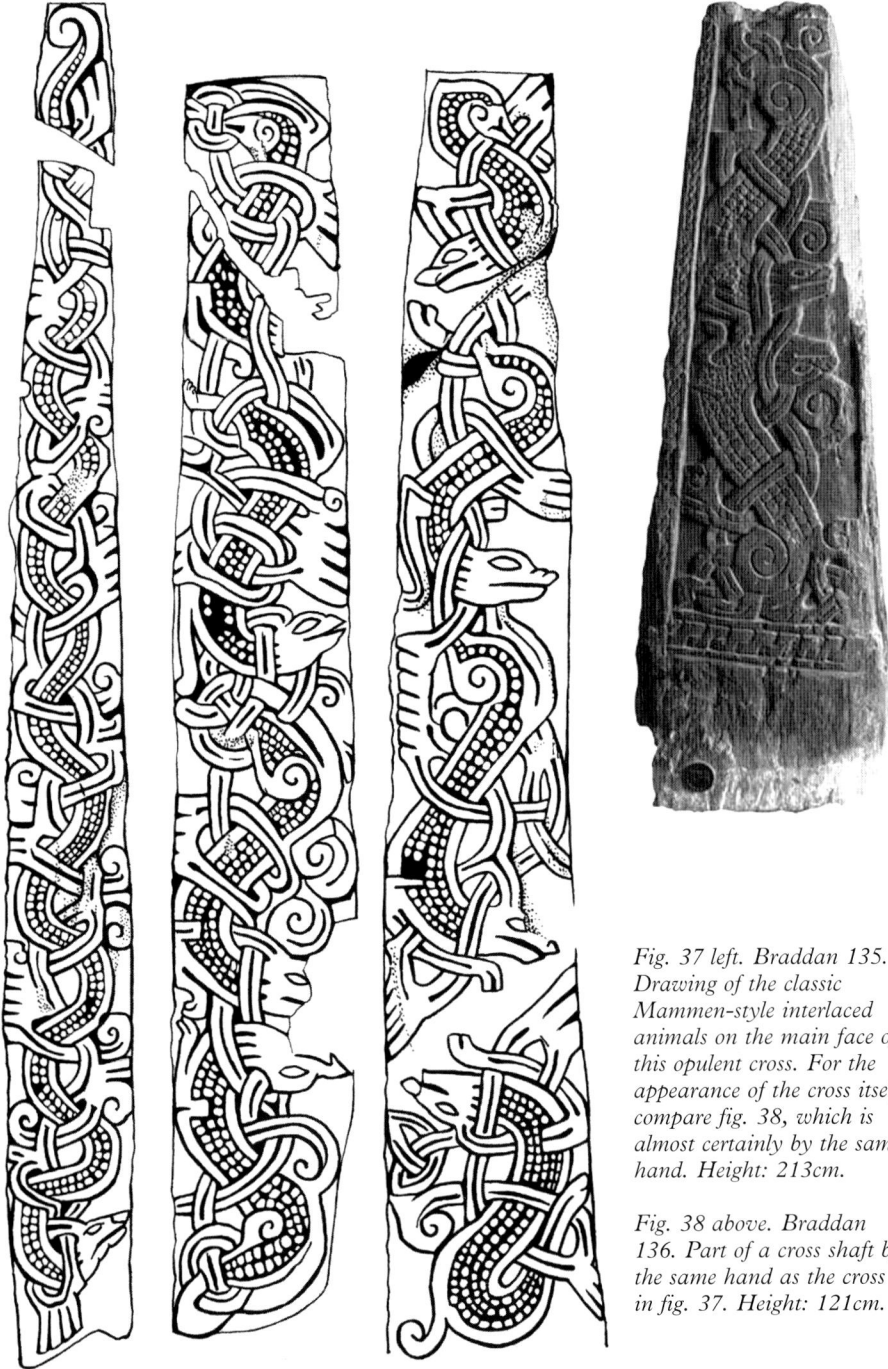

Fig. 37 left. Braddan 135. Drawing of the classic Mammen-style interlaced animals on the main face of this opulent cross. For the appearance of the cross itself compare fig. 38, which is almost certainly by the same hand. Height: 213cm.

Fig. 38 above. Braddan 136. Part of a cross shaft by the same hand as the cross in fig. 37. Height: 121cm.

The Jellinge style

This style takes its name from the ornament on a small silver cup from a grave in a mound at the royal centre of Jelling, Denmark, which is dated dendrochronologically to before 958/9. The style itself, however, has its origin at the beginning of the century. The chief motif is a sinuous quadruped with a round eye, pigtail and lip-lappet. The body of the animal and the pigtail frequently interlace together, and often interlace with similar elements of another animal. In its pure form the style is rare in the Island, but is best seen on the shaft of the cross on one face of Malew 120 (fig. 36).

The Mammen style

The Jellinge and Mammen styles overlap markedly, and were at one time considered to be different elements of the same style. They were only finally subdivided for convenience in 1966, and continue to be so labelled. The Mammen style takes its name from an iron axe, the faces of which are inlaid with silver wire, excavated from a Danish mound burial constructed in 970/1, which helps to date the style. On one face of the axe is an elongated foliate motif, the pelleted fronds of which spread from tight spiral bases without axiality across the whole face in an apparently untidy, but actually controlled, pattern. The fronds have curled hook-like ends; curved bites break the contour. On the other face is a bird with a round eye, a double-contoured substantial pelleted body and spiral hips, all caught up in frond-like tendrils, which spring from its wings and crest.

The Manx version of the Mammen style may best be seen on two free-standing crosses (one of which survives only as part of the shaft) from Braddan (135 and 136), which are clearly carved by the same hand. The sinuous animal caught up in interlace on the narrow face of no. 135 (fig. 37) is reminiscent of the rather more strictly separated animals of the Jellinge style. The slightly more robust animals on the broader faces and on no. 136 (fig. 38) are more typical of the Mammen style. The pelleting which fills the body is an important element of the style and is most clearly to be seen carved in walrus ivory or antler on a number of objects of high value; for example, filling the bodies of birds and animals on a remarkable walrus ivory casket originally in the treasury of Bamberg Cathedral, an object traditionally said to have belonged to a Danish princess, Kunigunde, wife of the emperor Henry II. While the dates of princess and axe do not match, the prestige of this long tradition indicates the importance and

Fig. 39. Kirk Michael 117. The animals in the panels below the head of the cross have the typical pointed eye and lip-lappet of the Ringerike style (the motif is repeated in the similar position on the other face of the cross). Height: 138cm.

Fig. 40. Kirk Michael 116. The animal with the the large body has a Ringerike-style eye, characteristically with its point towards the snout. Height: 39cm.

probable Danish origin of the object. The Braddan crosses are remarkable for their skilled craftsmanship and, being expensively elaborate, must both have been carved, like many others in the Island, in memory of people of high status (their names being recorded in runes on the stones). The Mammen style is otherwise rarely found in the Island, but does occur on a number of other stones (e.g. Kirk Michael 129, at the base of Kirk Michael 132, fig. 55, p.116, and on Braddan 138), which may indicate a date for them late in the series of Manx crosses.

The Ringerike style

The latest Scandinavian style to appear in the Isle of Man is the Ringerike style, which appears on two crosses from Kirk Michael (116; fig. 40, and 117; fig. 39) and on one face of Maughold 122 (fig. 41 right), which presumably date from the first half of the eleventh century. The style takes its name from a sandstone district of south-east Norway, where the style was used for a group of runic-inscribed slabs. The distinctive feature of the very different animals on the first two of these three stones is the pear- or

Fig. 41. Maughold 122. From Ramsey. One of the Sigurd crosses. Left: Otr is spread-eagled at the base, Regin is surrounded by his tools at top left. Right: the interlaced serpent in Ringerike form possibly represents Fáfnir. Height: 117cm.

almond-shaped eye, its 'point' facing towards the snout. One face of
Maughold 122 (fig. 41 right) is partially filled by an axially-disposed beast,
with its now much worn head top right. The disposition of this beast is also
typical of the Ringerike style, but is also to be seen in the Mammen style.
The main double-contoured creature is caught up in a complex interlace,
its head almost lost amongst its tendrils. In more disciplined form it is not
unlike the motif on a stone from Alstad, Norway, which is carved in the
Ringerike sandstone; the motif is also on to be seen on such Irish objects
as the earliest part of the shrine of the Cathach, as well as on a series of
mounts from the south of England. It is rarely encountered in the north of
England, but does occur in classic form on a slab from Otley, Yorkshire. In
the Western Isles it appears on a memorial slab from Dòid Mhàiri on Islay.
The style also appears on an unfinished cast gold ring from Greeba, which
was almost certainly made in the Island.

In the course of the late tenth and early eleventh centuries direct
Scandinavian stylistic influences apparently waned in the Island. The
Ringerike style in its pure form, for instance, appears on only these three
stones and a single unfinished gold ring. The other styles remained popular and even merged into each other, as is particularly to be seen on two
crosses from Braddan (135 and 136; figs. 37 and 38), where Jellinge and
Mammen stylistic traits appear side by side. Ballaugh 106 (fig. 33) demonstrates the strength of the Borre style, which, in a more lush version of
detail, introduces Mammen-style billeting. It would seem that as the settlers and their sculptors became more confident, they were able to blend
successfully elements of the Borre, Mammen and Ringerike styles.

Influences

The final Scandinavian style of the Viking Age, the Urnes style, which
dates in rough terms from 1050-1125, takes its name from the elaborate
carving on the re-used timbers of the earliest phase of a wooden stave-
church from western Norway. It does not appear in the Isle of Man. It is,
however, important in relation to the Manx series in providing negative evidence which indicates that the end date of Scandinavian ornament on
Manx crosses is signalled by the Ringerike elements on the Kirk Michael
and Maughold stones (above), which were possibly carved at the end of the
tenth or more probably at the beginning of the eleventh century. The
Urnes style, while known in the British Isles, was soon swallowed up by the
Romanesque style, newly-imported from the Continent. Although it is not
encountered in the Western Isles or in mainland Scotland, it was popular

in a more variant form in Ireland. It occurs in England on a gilt-bronze openwork brooch from Pitney, Somerset, and on the so-called crozier of Bishop Flambard found in a tomb in Durham Cathedral. More importantly, as some such metalwork could have been imported, its influence is apparent in architectural sculpture at Jevington in Sussex, on capitals in Kirkburn parish church in east Yorkshire and at Norwich; possibly also on a stone panel in the minster church at Southwell, Nottinghamshire.

Some ornamental elements similar to those used in the Island are found in nearby Cumbria. The remarkable standing cross from Gosforth (fig. 26) with its varied decoration combines the Borre style ring-chain and imaginative local derivatives of it, together with scenes from Scandinavian mythology and Christianity. But this cross is *sui generis* in almost all its aspects. The Borre ring-chain on the Muncaster cross (the only really convincing parallel to the Manx motif) has already been mentioned, but the style does not occur on the Gallowegian stones. It is difficult to say whether Cumbria provided the inspiration for the style's appearance in the Isle of Man or vice versa; the ubiquity of the pattern in the Island, however, and the rarity of true parallels in Cumbria would probably argue for the latter. The almost muddled aspect of the interlacing beasts on a cross-shaft from Great Clifton and on a tombstone from Gosforth, perhaps relate to the Jellinge style, but not convincingly so, and are in no way as directly derived as the animal on Malew 120 (fig. 36). A stone from Plumbland, Cumbria, is the only major north-west English example of a Jellinge-style motif. Derivatives of the Jellinge and Mammen styles may, however, have been influenced from sculpture of the earlier Scandinavian settlement of Yorkshire, where there are a number of good possible prototypes, which may explain the apparent lack of purity of style in the Cumbrian examples.

It is remarkable that styles on the Manx crosses faithfully follow those of the Scandinavian homeland. In this respect, with a few exceptions, they differ from the versions of the same styles found in England and Ireland, which are generally less pure. On this basis it seems evident that in the tenth century the Island was in close contact with Norway, as it was to be in political and religious terms until the collapse of Norwegian power after the Treaty of Perth in 1266, when the sovereignty of the Kingdom of Man and the Isles passed to Scotland.

A detailed study of the ornament shows that decorated standing memorial stones had ceased to be used in the Isle of Man by the second quarter of the eleventh century. The reasons for this are complicated and are discussed below (p.122ff).

Scandinavian mythology and other historiated images

The clearest and most remarkable signs of Scandinavian influence in the Island are the scenes taken from Scandinavian mythology carved on the memorial crosses. The stories on which the scenes are based otherwise survive only in thirteenth-century or later written sources, and derive from oral tradition of a period in which literacy in Scandinavia was confined to runic epigraphy. The earliest pictorial records of these narratives in Scandinavia are to be seen in representations of them on sculpture in wood and stone, supplemented by a few amulets probably depicting gods, presumably worn for protection. The symbolism of many amulets is sometimes regarded sceptically by students, but one such representation in particular has received general, if not universal, acceptance – a pendant in the form of the hammer of Thor, god of thunder and the protector of heroes, an image much used by today's 'pagans'. It must, however, be said that at least some of these 'hammers' could represent a T-shaped cross – the *tau* cross – which in the early church was often used as a symbol of the cross of Christ, as on the stone from Ronaldsway (164; p.32 and fig. 15). Some amulets – very rarely found – appear to represent the gods themselves. Carved scenes from a limited group of myths occur on stone occasionally in Sweden, but are also known (rarely) in England and the Isle of Man. Representations of gods (as distinct from legendary heroes) are to be seen on a few Manx crosses, but their identity must be carefully and sceptically considered.

The Sigurd story

One of the most securely-identified heroic myths, which involves the intervention of the gods, is the story of Sigurd the Volsung, episodes from which are depicted in a number of media in Scandinavia and in the Scandinavian settlements of the British Isles between the tenth and twelfth centuries. Perhaps its earliest surviving appearance anywhere is on Manx crosses of the tenth century. The tale itself is related in various thirteenth-century sources in poetry and prose, and finally in the later medieval *Volsunga saga*. Sigurd is familiar to many as Siegfried, part of whose story appears in Wagner's *Rheingold,* a story which the composer warmed up, dramatically embellishing and strengthening the plot. His inspiration was the thirteenth-century Middle High German *Niebelungenlied*, which was based on central European traditions of events which took place in the Burgundian kingdom in the fourth and fifth centuries.

At some stage this strange tale became entwined with the Scandinavian story of Sigurd. An Anglo-Saxon parallel to the Sigurd story is in some of its parts so close that its eponymous hero Weland is often identified with Sigurd. There are similarities in that a smith, Weland, maker of swords with supernatural powers, is easily compared to Regin, the smith in the story of Sigurd; but other details of this story, in both the Old Norse *Poetic Edda* and in the *Prose Edda*, are ultimately different. The two stories, however, the Old Norse saga and the German *Lied*, must have a distant common source. On one famous Anglo-Saxon object, the early eighth-century Franks Casket, with its curious mixture of scenes from Germanic, Biblical and even Roman and Jewish sources, Weland appears in his smithy in a form which is almost – but not quite – interchangeable with some interpretations of Regin's smithy on stone carving in England and Sweden.

Interpretation of the discrete part of the story of Sigurd represented in the Island is inevitably complicated and oblique, partly because of the fragmentary nature of the stones. But as the sculptures provide the earliest known depictions of the hero, they have received a great deal of scholarly attention. The critical part of the story, as told in the *Prose Edda* and on the Manx crosses, can be summarised briefly if account is also taken of details which occur in the text of the much later *Vǫlsunga saga*.

Sigurd was a distant descendant of Odin and has for this reason been labelled by Turville-Petre as a 'demi-god'. In the part of the story that appears in the Manx sources his god-like features are not particularly evident; he is portrayed rather as a not very intelligent hero. Gods do appear in some quantity in the Sigurd story, although only one, Loki, the wicked, joking god, plays an important role in the Manx cycle.

The saga version goes something like this: there was a man called Hreidmar, who was a farmer and a bit of a magician. He had three sons, two of whom, Fáfnir and Otr, were shape-changers. One became a serpent and the other, as his name implies, an otter. The third son was a dwarf, Regin, who, like many dwarves in Germanic tales, was a skilled smith. Regin made a sword for Sigurd, his foster son. Otr, in his changed form, was discovered by Odin, Hoenir and Loki taking a bite out of a salmon, whereupon Loki threw a stone at Otr and killed him. The gods skinned the otter and took the skin and salmon with them. They showed their prize to their host that night, little realising that this man Hreidmar was Otr's father. Hreidmar then demanded that the gods redeem the killing by covering the skin with gold, which Loki was able to provide by stealing it from another dwarf, Andvari, a goldsmith. This was sufficient to pay off Otr's

Fig. 42. Andreas 121. Height: 68cm. Left: in the side panel (below) Sigurd slays the serpent Fáfnir. Above, he cooks Fáfnir's heart on a spit. Right: Gunarr in the snake-pit.

father (a ring with magical properties was left over from the booty and taken by Odin). The two surviving brothers demanded their share of the gold, but Hreidmar refused to pay up and was then killed by Fáfnir, who took the gold away and hid it in a cave, where – as a serpent – he guarded it. Regin, not unnaturally, did not like this fraternal coup and plotted revenge by persuading his foster son, Sigurd, to kill the serpent. Taking his horse Grani with him, Sigurd went off to do his filial duty.

Digging a pit in the ground, he lay in it and, when Fáfnir came out of his cave to drink at the river, stuck him with the sword from below and killed him. Regin then re-joined Sigurd and, planning to kill him and steal the gold, suggested that the hero should roast Fáfnir's heart. Sigurd roasted the heart and, testing the state of his cooking, burnt his finger and put the finger with some of the cooked blood into his mouth. The magical properties

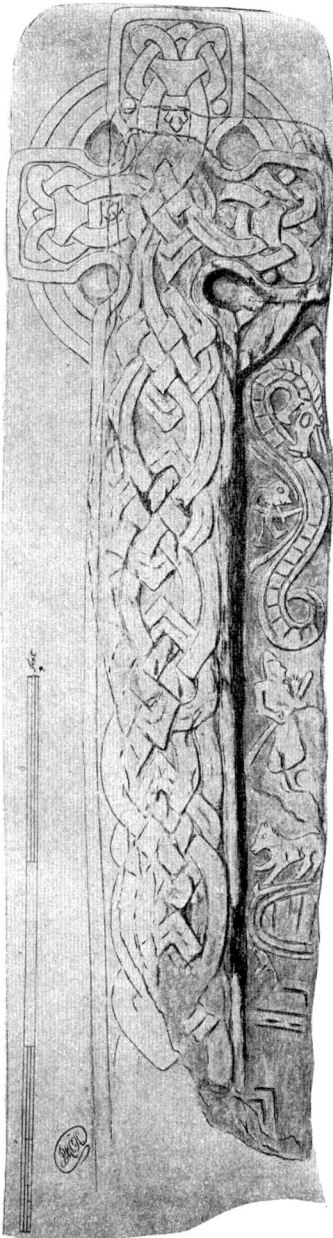

Fig. 43. Jurby 119. Sigurd slays the serpent Fáfnir. At the base of the panel is a possible representation of Fáfnir's empty cave. Height: 213cm.

in the serpent's blood enabled him to understand the language of the birds, who told Sigurd of Regin's intentions, advising him to behead his foster-father. Sigurd took this advice, beheaded Regin and went back to Fáfnir's lair, loaded the gold (Wagner's *Rheingold*) on Grani's back and rode off to the rest of his adventurous life, which need not concern us here.

Much of this action-packed story may be traced on five surviving, but much damaged, crosses in the Isle of Man, particularly on a stone from Ramsey (Maughold 122; fig. 41 right), but also on Malew 120 (fig. 36), Andreas 121 (fig. 42) and Jurby 119 (fig. 43), and possibly on Jurby 125 (fig. 44).

The earliest scenes of the central part of the Sigurd/Regin/Fáfnir cycle occur on one face of a stone from Ramsey (122; fig. 41 left), which shows some of the episodes. The cross is missing its head, although traces of its curved lower contour may just be seen on both faces. Squeezed into the right-hand corner of one face is a representation of a sword pommel of typical Scandinavian type. Regin's smith's tools (fig. 45) are scattered below it – bellows, tongs, anvil, hammers and a possible clamp or pair of shears, interspersed, as are all the images on the face of the Ramsey stone, with billets. The scattered billets probably represent, as suggested below, the gold treasure. The animal in the middle of the field is presumably Sigurd's horse, Grani, represented here as elsewhere with a pack on his back in which the hero had placed the

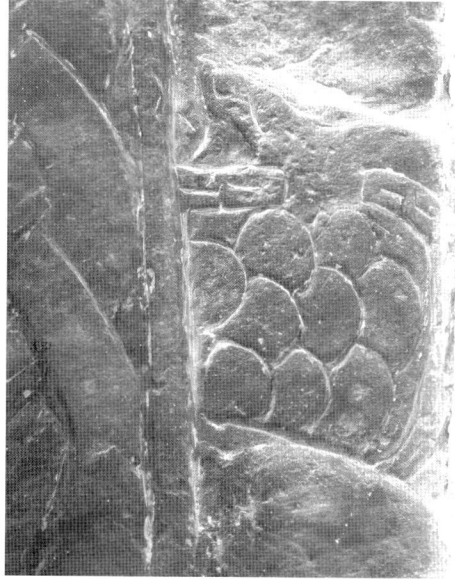

Fig. 44. Detail of Jurby 125.
To the right is Regin's cave
full of gold. Height: 79cm.

treasure. The only humanoid figure, bottom right, represents Loki in the act of throwing a rock to kill Otr, who is biting a great chunk out of a salmon. In the space between Grani and Otr is interlace, which probably represents the serpent Fáfnir. Caught up in the interlaced body is a spit on which are three doughnut-like objects, representing the serpent's heart as it was roasted by Sigurd; an element more clearly seen on two other Sigurd crosses (nos. 120; fig. 36 and 121; fig. 42 left), where Sigurd is shown cooking the spitted heart over a fire. Margeson queried the interpretation of this part of the story on no.122 (fig. 41 left) (see paper cited in bibliog-

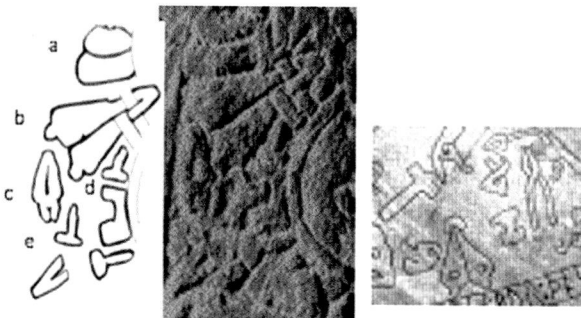

*Fig. 45. Regin's tools on Maughold 122 (fig. 41) – **a**. sword pommel, **b**. bellows,*
***c**. tongs, **d**. anvil and hammers, **e**. possibly a clamp – for comparison (right), the*
tools as shown on the Swedish rock-engraving, Ramsundsberget (cf. fig. 46).

Fig. 46. Ramsundsberget, Södermanland, Sweden. Illustrates many of the elements of the story of Sigurd, Regin and Fáfnir. Sigurd is seen, bottom right, slaying the serpent Fáfnir, which forms a ribbon for the runic inscription. In the tree, above, the birds tell of Regin's treachery; to the left is Sigurd's horse, Grani, Further to the right, Sigurd, having burnt his finger while cooking Fáfnir's heart, listens to the birds. To the far left, the beheaded Regin lies beside his tools.

raphy). Such 'doughnuts', however, are standard in representations of the serpent's heart – most famously on the surviving early thirteenth-century portal from the demolished stave-church from Hylestad, Aust-Agder, Norway (now in the Museum of Cultural History, Oslo), which retails many of the details of the Sigurd/Regin cycle in top-quality Romanesque wood-carving.

The other face of Maughold 122 (fig. 41 right) is partially filled with an animal of Ringerike form. The billets between the loops of the beast are possibly representative of the gold which forms a central element of the Sigurd story and are shown filling the space between the figural scenes on the other face of the stone. A pile of such billets (presumably the treasure) at the base of one face of a cross fragment from Jurby (125; fig. 44) is enclosed in what is possibly the representation of the mouth of a cave (Fáfnir's lair). If more of this stone had survived we might have seen a representation of Fáfnir. Another representation of the cave – but with no visible gold – can be seen below the animal on the side panel of another stone from a keeill site at Ballaconley, Jurby 119 (fig. 43).

The central part of Sigurd's story – the killing of Fáfnir – is clearly shown on the same stone from Jurby and on Malew 120 (fig. 36). On both crosses the hero is seen killing the serpent from below. A complete rendering of this classic scene was carved in the eleventh century on the living rock at Ramsund, Södermanland, in Central Sweden (fig. 46), and on what is surely a bad copy of it nearby at Gök, Södermanland. In both carvings are representations of Sigurd with his thumb in his mouth after burning his fingers while cooking Fáfnir's heart, although the heart is of a different form. On the same two rock-carvings Regin is shown beheaded (a scene which does not occur on the Manx stones). The story of the treacherous Regin was clearly popular among a wide Scandinavian audience. The beheaded smith is most clearly seen at Ramsund, where the decapitated man lies among his scattered tools, which include an anvil, hammer and a pair of bellows. Sigurd's horse, Grani with his backpack, is tied to a tree, in the branches of which are the birds which had forewarned Sigurd of Regin's plans. The whole is framed by a great ribbon which contains a runic inscription recording the building of a bridge. At one end of the frame the encircling ribbon forming the serpent's body is knotted, from which is produced the creature's head. Below the serpent Sigurd is seen with raised sword piercing the creature's belly, as on the three Manx stones (119 and 120 and 121), where they attack an undulating snake from below.

But central Sweden is a long way from the Isle of Man, and it is likely that the story was imported into the Island from south-western Norway where wooden portals of at least five twelfth-century stave-churches were carved with an attention to detail more clearly displayed than on the more difficult raw material of the much earlier Manx stones. The parallels are striking and indicate that there was a long-standing pictorial canon, with only minor variations of this part of the Sigurd story throughout Scandinavia, of which the Manx stones are the earliest survivers.

Interestingly, Regin also appears on contemporary sculpture in Northumbria – most strikingly at Halton, Lancashire, and Kirby Hill in North Yorkshire (figs. 47 and 48). On the first Regin is shown in his smithy, while in the scene above he appears, headless, lying surrounded by tools and the sword he has made for Sigurd. On the Kirby Hill memorial the beheaded Regin is shown above the thumb-sucking Sigurd. A similar scene occurs on a much-worn recumbent slab from York Minster, where the finger-licking Sigurd is associated with a headless Regin and a possible figure of Regin in his smithy. On one side of this slab a man with a sword raised as if to kill Fáfnir is depicted between two snake-like creatures; this is almost certainly Sigurd, although the story has been corrupted in the telling. Optimism has sometimes tempered the interpretation of other scenes in this region. Part of a cross-head from Ripon Cathedral, however, although fragmentary, appears to portray Sigurd with his hand to his mouth, tasting Fáfnir's blood. This and one or two other scenes with a fin-

Fig. 47 (above). Detail of a cross-shaft from Halton in Lancashire. Regin is shown in his workshop, surrounded by his tools, including bellows at the bottom of the panel.

Fig. 48 (right). Upper portion of a cross-shaft built into the parish-church wall at Kirby Hill, North Yorkshire. Height: 60cm. The beheaded Regin lies above; below him Sigurd licks his exaggerated thumb after learning of Regin's threatened betrayal.

ger-sucking figure are presumably representative of Sigurd, but others rely on imaginative interpretation, as is the case with a cross-shaft on a stone from Kilmorie, near Stranraer, Galloway. There is a possible representation of Regin surrounded by his tools on a stone from Iona; but the scene, which includes a ship with figures, is muddled. The identification of so-called Sigurd scenes on the side of a hog-backed tombstone from Heysham, Lancashire, was rejected by Margeson, but has since been re-born. The images are, however, so far away from normal Sigurd iconography that it is now generally dismissed from the canon.

It is not hard to understand the relevance of the Sigurd and Regin story to Christianity. There are obvious parallels in biblical sources and in Christian legend which could be used by a preacher in exegetic mode, addressing the newly-converted, or still to be baptised, audience. Chief is the idea of the dragon-slayer as a Christian hero, to be compared to the Archangel Michael (as told in the Book of Revelations 12.7-9, where Michael and his angels kill a dragon). The imagery had gained importance during the reign of the Emperor Constantine in the early fourth century, when the emperor is known to have used it as an image in celebrating a major victory. The symbol of Michael slaying the dragon (representing evil) was popular from that time forward, and is now well bedded in the iconography of the Christian church. The tasting of Fáfnir's blood has been taken by some to symbolise, in a rather labyrinthine fashion, the Eucharist, but this seems rather fanciful.

Another story linked to the Sigurd cycle, but one not so easily related to Christian iconography, is told in one of the early poems. It tells of a mythical hero, Gunnar, a blood brother of Sigurd, who, like most of the figures in the story, also lusted after the treasure. So he arranged for his younger brother to kill Sigurd. After the usual amount of gore, Gunnar, the only survivor who knew where the treasure was hidden, was bound and dropped into a pit full of poisonous serpents. Here he was pretty helpless but managed, by striking up a tune with his toes on his harp (kindly provided by his wife), to send the snakes to sleep so that they could then be killed. To no avail, for Gunnar was stung to death by a large and ugly adder, which had managed to survive the slaughter. General mayhem followed, but by the end of the tale the treasure had been buried in the Rhine and was thus lost forever. It is possible that a bound, but harp-less, Gunnar is represented on one of the Manx Sigurd crosses (Andreas 121; fig. 42 right). He is certainly bound and is surrounded by snakes – but there is no harp, so the identification has been queried, although his presence on the reverse face of the stone of scenes of Sigurd and Fáfnir make such an identification plausible. A harpist is shown on a cross from Kirk Michael (no. 130), but here the figure almost certainly represents David, the Old Testament king and psalmist and a popular subject elsewhere in the contemporary Christian world, especially in Ireland and Pictland – particularly as he is shown above two clerics, probably bishops, their hands raised in blessing, carrying croziers with *tau*-shaped heads.

A great deal of academic ink has been spilt attempting to identify

Scandinavian deities and heroes on other Manx crosses. Particularly unconvincing has been the attempt to see the god Thor on the almost complete slab, Bride 124. Kermode attempted to identify a number of persons and scenes amid the very coarsely-carved ornament plastered over both faces of this almost undamaged cross. Amidst the ornament he identified scenes from Ragnarǫk, as well as characters such as Svanhildr, and Thor, carrying an ox-head in his hand on his way to go fishing with Hymir. Margeson clearly demonstrated that there is no element of reality in his convoluted interpretation of the figures on this stone and suggested, very tentatively, that some of the figures have a Christian meaning, but even this is doubtful. Thor, who has been much discussed, was a popular hero in the nineteenth century when Kermode was doing his ground-breaking work, and Kermode may well have had his vision coloured by the discovery of a stone at Gosforth in Cumbria which is clearly an interpretation of the fabled account of Thor fishing for, and hooking, the Midgard serpent, which circled the world. The scene on the Gosforth slab is closely paralleled iconographically in Scandinavia as far away as Uppland in Sweden, and at Hunnestad, Skåne, in what was then Denmark. The Bride cross, however, bears no relationship to such scenes.

Ragnarǫk and the Resurrection

Odin, chief of the gods, is, however, perhaps represented on Jurby 125, where a hanged man is carried away by a spear-bearing figure. This is possibly Odin, as hanged men for complicated reasons belong to him. But this is a unique representation on a fragmentary cross. and its interpretation has been met with scepticism. A representation of Odin on one face of a fragment of a cross-slab from Andreas (128; fig. 49 left) is, however, accepted as such by almost all scholars and is set in relationship to Christ on the other face (fig. 49 right). Here a Christian idea, the coming of Christ and the resurrection of the dead, is set in apposition to the pagan idea of Ragnarǫk, the doom of the gods and the end of the old world.

Ragnarǫk is mentioned frequently in the early poetry and prose of the North. The causes which lead to its conclusion are complicated and need not concern us in detail here; a summary will suffice. The world of the gods is threatened by a great tidal wave and the forces of the fire-demon Surt and the fearsome wolf, Fenrir, whose open jaws encompass the whole world and beyond. Odin orders Heimdall to blow a horn to summon his forces to fight the attackers; there is great slaughter, but for the gods the

Fig. 49. Andreas 128. Both faces of the fragment of a cross-slab. Left: Odin being swallowed by the wolf Fenrir. Right: the risen Christ tramples the snakes. Height: 35cm.

fight is hopeless, and as Odin is swallowed by Fenrir the whole world and the dwelling of the gods is burnt up. A second fertile earth will now appear from the sea, the details of which are vague and contradictory.

On one face of the Andreas stone we see Odin, carrying his spear, in the process of being devoured by Fenrir. On his shoulder is one of his raven familiars and behind him is a coiled snake. On the other face Christ, the harbinger of a renewed life after the end of the world, is shown risen and trampling a snake under foot, as foretold in Psalm 91, '…you shall step on asp and cobra and shall tread safely on snake and serpent…'. To affirm that the prophecy has been fulfilled, a fish, a secret symbol of Christ derived from the anagram of his name in Greek (ἰχθνς), is seen beside the figure of

Fig. 50. Jurby 127. Detail. This has been interpreted as Heimdall summoning the gods to battle at Ragnarǫk.

the risen Christ, who is carrying a cross and a book (a reference to the Bible as the word of God). The contrast between the dying Odin and the living Christ is thus very neatly made. As an aside it should be mentioned that the association of Christ with Odin has long been noted. The similarity between the two is more pointed in that both hung on a tree, Christ at Calvary and Odin on Yggdrasil, the tree of fate (on which he had hanged himself for nine days – hence hanged men as well as those who had died in battle belonged to him).

The two scenes of juxtaposition seen on the Andreas fragment do not appear elsewhere in Manx iconography, although crudely-carved scenes of Christ trampling on snakes do occur in Northumbria, as at Burton-in-Kendal, Cumbria (where Christ is again portrayed carrying a cross), and on a number of other English crosses. In rather more finished fashion, on High Crosses in Ireland (at Durrow, Co. Offaly, the risen Christ appears on the cross-head itself carrying a cross and a flowering rod – normal symbols of the resurrection – standing above a rather tidy interlaced snake). The claim that Ragnarǫk appears as an apparent graffito on a block of Magnesian limestone in the church at Skipwith, East Yorkshire, is difficult to swallow as it is so coarsely drawn. It must await further evaluation.

A possible reference to Ragnarǫk is perhaps to be seen at the head of the cross on Jurby 127, where a man wearing a sword and blowing a long horn appears (fig. 50). This was identified by Kermode as Heimdall, watchman of the gods, sounding his horn (*Gjallarhorn* – 'the ringing horn') to summon the gods to their final battle. The only other suggested representations of Heimdall in the British Isles are on the Gosforth cross in Cumbria and, more doubtfully, on a cross-shaft from Norbury, Derbyshire. But this interpretation may be false, and the figure on the Jurby slab could refer to the passage in 1 Corinthians, 52, 'For the trumpet shall sound and the dead shall be raised, immortal, and we shall be changed', in which case the figure might represent the Archangel Michael, who, according to early medieval legend, heralds the second coming of Christ. In this age of religious syncretism the parallel with Heimdall might well have been drawn by a priest in his homily. Indeed such might well have been the purpose behind the presence of other seemingly irrelevant scenes drawn from Scandinavian mythology, which occur on Christian monuments during a period of conversion in the Island and elsewhere.

Christian iconography

As one struggles with the interpretation of non-Christian scenes on the Manx cross-slabs, it is almost too easy to forget that these are monuments raised by Scandinavians on the cusp of conversion, memorialised on stones, the chief motif of which is the Christian cross itself. Yet Christ himself rarely appears on the Manx crosses of this period, although his name is invoked in a runic inscription (see below, p.136).

The carved stone Rushen 61 (fig. 51) was found on the Calf of Man in the mid-eighteenth century, and was finally purchased by the Manx Museum in 1956. The slab is carved on a single face, of which part is missing. No record survives of its actual find-place and, despite searches carried out for more than 150 years, no trace has been found of the missing part of the stone; nor has any evidence of a likely setting for it been discovered. It is the only Manx stone to provide a complete representation of Christ, with some of the normal iconographical detail of the period. It is a well-carved piece of fine-grained local, mudstone-siltstone decorated, on one side only, with a panel which portrays a stylised Crucifixion. A plain footing below the carved panel suggests that it was originally let into the ground and it could, therefore, be either an altar frontal or the side panel of a tomb, like that excavated at Ronaldsway (164; fig. 15). A bearded, long-haired Christ is shown nailed to the cross. His forehead is marked with the letter *omega* and there are spirals at his shoulders. His robes are formalised in panels and he wears a circular breast-plate decorated with a double-stranded interlace, while an interlace motif of four separate loops appears below it. The feet are seen laid out flat, each showing the head of a nail. On one side of Christ is Longinus with a spear, while the figure of Stephaton, the sponge-bearer, which was presumably on Christ's left, is broken away and is now missing.

This stone is completely out of series with the other Scandinavian-period stones on the Island, and is unique in the Island. For a long time it was thought to be of eighth- or ninth-century date, when such images were known elsewhere in England and Ireland. The image of Christ portrayed here is almost certainly derived from a later Irish source, as, for example, from an illuminated Irish manuscript like the eleventh-century *Southampton Psalter* (St John's College, Cambridge C.9, fol. 38v). Although crucifixion scenes appear on the heads of a number of Irish High Crosses, variations of detail – particularly of dress – are marked. The whole composition of the Calf crucifixion is best paralleled on a series of bronze plaques (from books or shrines) of Irish origin, which are usually dated to the eighth or ninth century; but its closest parallel, as

Fig. 51. Rushen 61. The crucifixion of Christ. Height: 66cm.

Fig. 52. Kirk Michael, Michael 129. Left: the
crucifixion of Christ, with a cock and an angel flanking the cross-head. Right: the reverse

Fig. 53. Cross-
head from
Kirklevington,
North Yorkshire.
Height: 43cm.

was argued in an unpublished paper by Basil Megaw, is to be found on a
copper-alloy plaque from near Clonmacnoise, Co. Offaly, which is slightly
out of series, but has incidental ornament in the Ringerike style and is
therefore to be dated to the late tenth century, a date which chimes with
the interlace on Christ's breast-plate. Like the plaque, the Calf stone portrays Christ with a forked beard, while the supporting figure is seen in pro-
file. The spirals are very similar to those on the wings of angels on the Irish
mount. An interesting, but much more crudely-carved, stone panel depict-

ing the Crucifixion probably came from Penrith, Cumbria, and is quite closely paralleled to the Calf panel; it has been dated by Bailey to the tenth century.

The figure of a crucified Christ filling a cross-head is rarely encountered in the British Isles in the tenth century, but in Ireland he appears in this position on some of the great High Crosses; for example on the west face of the cross of Muiredach at Monasterboice, Co. Louth. Apart from a rather faint and hardly noticeable figure among the muddled decoration on Maughold 98, only a single representation of the crucifixion – which might also refer to his resurrection or to Christ's second coming – appears on a cross-head of a normal Scandinavian-period stone in the Isle of Man, from the churchyard at Kirk Michael (129; fig. 52 left). It is possible – because so many crosses have been decapitated – that other images of Christ did at one time exist on the Manx crosses. However, such images are also rare in tenth-century Northumbria, although the head of a cross from Kirklevington, Yorkshire (fig. 53), provides the best, if more crudely carved, parallel to the Kirk Michael Christ. On both stones the arms are outstretched, and snakes appear as fillers on the cross-arms. On Kirklevington, the snakes are represented as tidy interlace motifs, with a head below Christ's armpit, while on the Kirk Michael stone the interlacing snakes are more elaborately carved and are bound with a ring (the other face of the cross-head is covered with interlace, with unidentifiable animals in each corner). Other examples of snakes surrounding a figure with outstretched arms (here totally enclosing it) occur on the head of a cross found at Durham (no. 5) on the site of the chapter-house of the cathedral, and (not on a cross-head) possibly portrayed on the side of a hogback tombstone, at Sockburn, Co. Durham (no. 21). While the crucifixion is pictured quite often in Ireland, there are only a handful of such images in Wales and Scotland.

In discussing the Kirk Michael stone, Kermode suggested that the figure with arms outstretched in blessing represents the ascension of Christ. On the other hand, the cock on the top left of the cross-head (fig. 52 left) would more probably indicate the second coming of Christ. Indeed, in some versions of this story, the cock signals the second coming, when Christ tramples the snakes. Balancing the cock on the right side of the head is an angel. Of the three interpretations – the crucifixion, the ascension and the second coming of Christ – the first appears unlikely; the second lacks iconographical clues; while the last seems a reasonable guess, and is at least

Fig. 54. Maughold 79, from Keeill Chiggyrt. Possibly
representing Christ. Height: 86cm.

paralleled in part with the resurrection of Christ on the cross fragment from
Andreas (128; fig. 49 right) discussed above.

One image, often interpreted as being of Christ, dominates the shaft of a
wheel-headed cross from Keeill Chiggyrt, Maughold (79; fig. 54). The
head of the cross is unusual in that the arms are formed of various interlace

patterns of Viking-Age date, which expand slightly from a central roundel to meet the rolled edge which borders the circle. Unusually, the spaces between the arms of the cross are left plain. The shaft of the cross-slab, which tapers towards its foot, is dominated by a bearded figure with hunched shoulders and arms hanging from the elbows towards the bowed legs.

The same image possibly occurs incidentally in a side panel among the very rough and muddled imagery on Bride 124, but is not known elsewhere in either Northumbria or Ireland. It has been related to the image of a figure of Christ on the shaft of a cross at Kirkby Stephen, Cumbria, which has the same hunched shoulders and hanging arms, but this figure is bound by rings on legs and arms. The figure on the Cumbrian stone, long known as a 'bound devil' (due to a misunderstanding of degenerate volutes one either side of the head of the figure) is generally, but not universally, agreed to be a figure of Christ, symbolising his struggle with the devil. It is perhaps related to the bound Christ on the great tenth-century royal monument at Jelling in Denmark, and to a (now headless) figure bound with snakes on a bone carving in the Mammen style from the Thames at London. Other suggestions as to this symbolism have been advanced, but the lack of clear iconographic parallels suggests that the identification of the Kirkby Stephen image as Christ is correct, and that the parallel of stance with the figure on the Maughold stone makes such an interpretation plausible.

Most of the Scandinavian-period memorials on the Island are dominated by the cross – the chief Christian symbol throughout the ages – but without a representation of Christ. It seems as though at this period Christ was not allowed to be portrayed iconographically, or that the monument itself is a symbolical representation of the empty cross after the deposition of Christ. Thus it might be possible to interpret a small figure above the right-hand arm of the cross on one face of Kirk Michael 129 (fig. 52 right) as Christ ascending to heaven. A detail of the figure, which missed Kermode's eagle eye on his drawing in *Manx Crosses*, is an incised cross on his body. His right hand is apparently raised in blessing and it is just possible that on the much-damaged corner of the cross above the man's head are the tail feathers of a bird (a dove is often seen above the cross in later Christian iconography). In similar positions on the other face of the cross are two symbols associated with the crucifixion story, a cock and an angel. This interpretation is a bow drawn at a venture and nothing more!

In a previous chapter (p.47) it has been pointed out that at the foot of a number of slabs of both the pre-Scandinavian and Scandinavian periods in the Island there are out-turned spirals which may be related to the image of the cross as a tree, an idea familiar in the liturgy. The idea of the cross as a tree is basic to one of the most moving poems in Anglo-Saxon litera-ture, *The Dream of the Rood*, in which the cross itself recounts the suffering of Christ, the young hero, on a tree. Part of the text of this poem is carved in Anglo-Saxon runes on the mid-eighth-century cross from Ruthwell, Dumfriesshire, which, with its complicated inward iconography, is one of the most elaborate Christian monuments to survive from this period of Northumbrian greatness and ecclesiastical influence.

The most remarkable Manx version of the cross with spirals at its foot occurs on Kirk Michael 132 (fig. 55). It is well carved and, on the basis of the Mammen-style animals at its foot, must date from the late tenth cen-tury. On one face the cross has spirals on either side of the shaft below the head and at its foot. Below the two former spirals are smaller secondary crosses, carefully constructed from ribbons, the shafts of which are formed of a double ribbon which splits at the foot to return at a pointed loop over a straight horizontal beaded line. It might be possible to interpret their proximity and position as images of the crosses on either side of the cross of Christ at Calvary (Luke 23. 33). Such a combination of symbols is encountered (less elaborately as three *tau* crosses) on the pre-Scandinavian slab from Ronaldsway (Malew 164; fig. 15), a combination also known from Kirkmadrine and Whithorn in Galloway, long associated with the Island. The three crosses on the Kirk Michael stone could thus be seen as depicting the crosses as trees.

Meaning – symbols or narrative?

While the interpretation (outlined above, pp.106-8) of the identity of the two figures on Andreas 128 (fig. 48 and 49) as Christ and Odin has occa-sionally been questioned, the argument seems to be reasonable. We would be less secure of the suggested interpretation in Christian terms of the rep-resentation of figures from the Sigurd cycle – Sigurd, Fáfnir and Gunnar – on the Manx crosses if it were not for the presence of scenes from the same cycle carved on the portals of the Norwegian stave-churches. It is, howev-er, hard to identify other figures carved on the crosses, although they would surely have had meaning to both the priest and his audience when they were first carved.

As an example of such uncertainty one might take the much discussed

figure of a woman on the fragment of a slab from Kirk Michael (123; fig. 56), who wears a long trailing dress, has long hair (curled at the ends) down her back and carries an object which has the appearance of an uprooted sapling, the roots being clearly represented and the crown being shown as two billets. The figure is possibly repeated on Jurby 125, where unfortunately the head is missing and the object carried is partly obscured by the clamp which now holds the stone in place. That she is a woman is demonstrated by her long trailing dress, which is closely related to that figured on the Kirk Michael stone and, according to Kermode's drawing of the stone before it was clamped, carries a somewhat similar staff or sapling before her. A woman on the fragment from Jurby 127, with her trailing dress and long hair, is the only other female figure known on the Island; she, however, carries no upright object in her extended hand.

These figures are often interpreted as valkyries (from the Old Norse *valr kjósa* literally 'chooser of the dead'). They were the servants of Odin who on the battlefield chose those who died to live with the god in his hall, Valhalla (*Valhǫll*). They welcomed the dead to the hall and provided them with drink. Credence is lent to this interpretation by the appearance of

Fig. 55. Kirk Michael 132. Wash drawing by P. M. C. Kermode. Possibly representing the three crosses on Calvary. Height (now visible): 235cm.

Fig. 56. Kirk Michael 123. Female figure. Height: 41cm.

women in every way similar in appearance to the images on the three Manx stones, save that they carry horns and not saplings or staves. They are possibly to be seen on a fragment of a much-damaged tapestry from the early ninth-century Viking ship-grave from Oseberg in south-west Norway, and on stone monuments of similar date or earlier from the Swedish island of Gotland, which portray them in association with halls (?Vallhalla). On the other hand valkyries, when they ride out for Odin to the battle-field, are said to carry spears. The identification of female spear-carriers on the reconstructed Oseberg tapestry, however, is very doubtful; the figures appear to be dressed as men and although spears do appear in front of two women, neither have hold of them. A woman on a fragment of another piece of tapestry from the same burial appears to hold a similar 'sapling' to

that on Kirk Michael 123, but the fragment is so damaged that, although
the sapling is clearly evident, the hand of the woman is missing.

The other interpretation of these figures is that they are seeresses, wise
women of god-like power of prophecy, who appear in one of the earliest
poems of the *Poetic Edda* (the *Vǫluspá*). Such interpretations are not alto-
gether trustworthy. There are two names for such women, one of which is
vǫlur, sometimes translated as 'staff-bearer', and the woman portrayed on
Kirk Michael 123 has been identified as such on the basis of what she holds
in her hand. There is evidence that a number of Scandinavian women's
graves of this period have such staffs, but the attempt to interpret such a
grave in Peel as a *vǫlur* is improbable, as the object is almost certainly a
cooking-spit. Some of the objects buried with women in Scandinavia may
indeed indicate the presence of seeresses, but in some cases the staff in the
grave may merely be a distaff, a typical woman's spinning tool and a symbol of her domestic authority.

A persistent presence on crosses of the Scandinavian period in the Isle of
Man is the deer. In most cases it is clearly an animal of the chase, with men
and dogs in pursuit (e.g. on Bride 124, Jurby 125 and Andreas 131; fig.
30), the dogs often appearing on the back of the stag. This latter motif ('the
hart and hound'), when it occurs alone and not as part of a hunting scene,
for example on Maughold 97 and Michael 130, must have been derived
from hunting scenes in Pictland, where it had its origin in Romano-British
images. In the tenth century the hart and hound motif occurs on contemporary crosses in Lancashire and Cheshire, at Lancaster and Neston, for
example, and elsewhere in England in the tenth century.

The stag is an important beast and appears in a number of symbolic guises in both Christian (as Christ) and Norse (as Odin) mythological texts.
But its meaning on the Manx crosses (as in Pictland) is obscure, although
bold attempts have been made to interpret them, of which the most likely
is the pursuit of Christianity (the stag) by the forces of evil (the dogs) – as
an image useful to a priest in exegesis. A few other animal images – boars,
goats, bull, wolf – on the Manx crosses are sometimes interpreted as
Christian (or indeed pagan) symbols. Although they doubtless had meaning to priest and audience, it is difficult to pin down their symbolism today.

Apart from the cross itself and rare depictions of the crucified Christ,
there are a number of minor symbols, some of which are obvious – for
example the angel who appears on one side of the cross-head of Kirk
Michael 129 and the cock (see above p.112ff) which appears on the other

side (fig. 52 left). But in similar positions on the other face of this cross (fig. 52 right), a serpent-like animal is opposed to a man, who may be carried off by a bird of prey (this part of the stone is damaged), the meaning of which is obscure. On the broken head of Jurby 127 in a similar position is a woman with a trailing dress (see above, p.115ff), whose presence cannot now be explained. It should be noted, however, that on the other face of the slab Heimdall is in a similar position.

Crosses of the Scandinavian period are dominated by interlace ornament. Even the running vegetal ornament on Kirk Michael 101 (fig. 32) and its more elaborate expression on Ballaugh 106 (fig. 33 right), based on the vine-scroll (see above p.88), have been developed into a simple interlace pattern. There are many serpentine animals on the Manx crosses (e.g. Kirk Michael 117, fig. 39; and Braddan 136, fig. 38) where any symbolic or narrative meaning has been lost. A specific interlace ornament, however, the triquetra (a regular triple-looped, compass-drawn ribbon motif) which appears before the Scandinavian period in the Island (e.g. on Maughold 42, fig. 16), is presumably derived from similar motifs common in England and Western Europe in the eighth and ninth centuries. On Scandinavian-period crosses in the Isle of Man it appears as one of four quadrants within a circle (e.g. on Kirk Michael 132; fig. 55). It also appears as a single figure immediately outside the ring of the cross. The triquetra is an ancient motif and although interpreted as a symbol of the Trinity, it appears to have first been interpreted in this guise only in the nineteenth century.

A great deal of ink has been spilled and a great deal of ingenuity has been involved in attempting to interpret the meaning of many of the motifs and scenes depicted on the Christian memorials in the Isle of Man. The evidence presented here has been stretched as far as it would seem reasonable and possible to go – and some might say further.

Colour – a footnote

In all the discussion of the ornament of the Manx crosses their colour has not been mentioned, although the stone of which they are made and decorated is frequently referred to. The type of stone – mudstone, granite, limestone and erratics – appears as different tones of grey and brown. But have these stones always been left plain? Close study of English stones carried out during the compilation of the Corpus of Anglo-Saxon Stone Sculpture (of which twelve out of fifteen volumes have now appeared) has revealed a few traces of paint. Complete schema of painting on stone have been recognised, chiefly on the internal faces of walls and on architectural detail, as at Deerhurst, Gloucestershire, where the paint was laid on prepared panels of ashlar. The lack of traces of paint on English monumental sculpture of this period is presumably due to the simple fact that most of these stones were originally erected in the open air and have been roughly handled over the centuries. Occasionally both casual and excavated finds have produced major clues, although none as complete as a decorated stone panel from the ancient churchyard of St Paul's Cathedral in London found in the early nineteenth century. On this panel of an early eleventh-century slab-made tomb (with a Scandinavian runic inscription on one edge), now in the Museum of London, a lion is painted in blue/black and red with carefully formed white spots; the lion is caught up in Ringerike-style interlace and set against a plain gesso ground, defined by a red border. A contemporary fragment of a grave-slab from St Maurice's church, Winchester, has a runic inscription highlighted in red paint (presumably red lead). In Northumbria such distinctive finds of colour are rare; there are, however, a few cases where traces of colour have been found. At York traces of gesso and colour have been found by careful examination of stones both in the Minster cemetery and at a couple of other sites. In Scandinavia, although traces of paint are rarely found, repairs to the church at Köping on the Swedish island of Öland from 1915 onwards have uncovered a large number of fragments of rune-stones, painted in red, black and white on a gesso background; thus for the first time, it has been demonstrated that many of the vast number of Swedish rune-stones of the eleventh century may have been painted in a similar fashion.

No traces of colour have yet been found on the Manx stones, probably because most of them had stood in the open air for many years and have been enthusiastically scrubbed by generations of amateur and professional scholars in search of decoration or inscriptions. Although many had been recovered from the walls of buildings in and around the churches or on neighbouring farms, similar opportunities have not offered themselves in the examination of more ancient buildings, churches or 'keeills'. Now that conservation is the first demand of the professional, it is to be hoped that such traces will be found on future finds. It must be assumed that stones were indeed painted in the Island and it might be that some of the stones with inscriptions and plain faces, as for example Onchan 141 and Marown 139, would have afforded opportunities to highlight the inscriptions, while other stones with complicated ornament could also have been painted.

The end of the sculptural tradition

Upright Manx memorial crosses clearly ceased to be produced in the early years of the eleventh century. It may be easy to say that a rather roughly executed and damaged cross-slab from Maughold (142; fig. 57) is the latest of the series to survive. The decoration is confined to a single cross on each face. Both crosses have an incised border with a cross-hatched contour giving the effect of a cable moulding. A series of rectangular interlocking linear pentagons fills the shafts of each cross. A runic inscription is divided between the two faces, along the side-panels of each cross.

The form of the crosses clearly belongs to the Scandinavian series and the layout of the slab might be compared, for example, to that of Onchan 141, save that the cross is not ring-headed. The stone has one extraordinary feature – a graffito of a ship with a single mast and furled sail, a beaked prow with high wash-strakes and a stern with side-rudder. While the ship could have been carved in outline by the same hand that cut the cross and the runes, it is more likely to have been a later graffito, representing a badge of the Lords of the Isles, first mentioned as being used by Rǫgnvaldr, King of Man and the Isles (died 1229). It later appears as an heraldic device of a number of later medieval Scottish

Fig. 57. Maughold 142. One of the latest memorial crosses from the Island. The single-masted ship with furled sail is probably a graffito. Height: 76cm.

chieftains, those of the MacKinnons, for example, whose Iona tombstones bear similar heraldic representations of ships. Neither the ornament nor the runic inscription can definitely indicate the final phase of the Manx crosses; on general grounds only it might be dated in the eleventh century, although it is possible that the incised ship is a later addition, perhaps even indicating a secondary use of the slab.

An interesting footnote to the series of crosses is provided by two undecorated stones – clearly not memorials – from the parish of Maughold (no. 144 from Cornaa, some 4-5km from Maughold church where no. 145, fig. 62, was found). The former is the first text produced on the Island to record the name of a priest, Juan/John, who inscribed the stone and on which he states that he lived in the Cornaa valley. Juan also carved the other stone, which not only has a runic inscription, but also an exercise in the ogam alphabet. The Cornaa stone must be dated, at the earliest, to the late twelfth century as it the records the name of a saint, Malachi, known to have died in 1148. Juan was clearly a man of antiquarian tendencies!

To attempt to understand the circumstances in which, theoretically, the practice of raising memorial stones in the Isle of Man ceased, it is important to understand the Church's growing interest in controlling burial elsewhere in Europe. As elsewhere in Europe, burial in the Isle of Man seems to have been unregulated outside the monastic sites until the ninth century. The dead could be buried and commemorated in what amounted to private familial or community cemeteries. In the ninth and tenth century the Church within the Carolingian Empire began to insist that the clergy control the burial of the dead. This insistence on ecclesiastical control was soon eagerly embraced by the Church in England. Regulations, for example, were introduced to guide bishops in the consecration of graveyards – there was presumably more money in such practices for the Church than in the previously unregulated burial in family or community-organised graveyards. As a consequence of these reforms local churches – 'field churches' or chapels – began to be constructed by patronage of the local landowners which could be served by clergy initially from the major – non-monastic – churches in England (known as minsters).

These new simple structures in many cases developed into the medieval parish churches, as more priests became available. For some time the western regions of the British Isles retained the old unhallowed burial practices in cemeteries, often – as in the Isle of Man – without associated buildings, and, where such buildings did exist (the keeills), many did not develop into parish churches (see discussion above, p.17).

There are good reasons, therefore, for suggesting that the cessation of the practice of raising standing monuments was in part based on the ecclesiastical reforms (including clerical control of burials and cemeteries) of the tenth and eleventh centuries. In areas where standing stone crosses were raised in greatest numbers, particularly in Northumbria, Cumbria and parts of the Midlands, but also in such non-Anglian areas as Scotland and the Isle of Man, the practice ceased almost abruptly in the early years of the eleventh century. The evidence of the stylistic history of stone sculpture demonstrates this indubitably, a fact clearly indicated by the absence of the latest Scandinavian style – the Urnes style – on the crosses in the areas of Scandinavian settlement, and the rarity of the Ringerike style which, as in the Island, occurs on only two or three examples in Northumbria and Scotland. Standing memorial crosses seem to have gone out of fashion, perhaps on clerical instruction, and only a few, following a different tradition and form, were raised in County Clare, in the far west of Ireland.

In some areas of Britain the standing memorials were replaced by recumbent stone slabs, not unlike those from Govan (see above, p.72), which sealed an individual burial and were decorated with simple ornament. These are especially evident also in the eastern Danelaw, particularly in Lincolnshire and Cambridgeshire, where oblong stones decorated with simple interlace and cruciform patterns are decorated on one face and the long sides only. These are dated (some by excavation) between the late tenth and late eleventh centuries. In some of these areas they are associated with vertical grave-markers, as at St Mark's church in the city of Lincoln. These Lincolnshire slabs parallel those of a slightly earlier date excavated in situ under the floor of York Minster, between the head and foot-stones of some of which are long horizontal slabs, some made of re-used Roman ashlars which often do not cover the length of the grave.

In Scandinavian Cumbria and western Yorkshire (and in a few outlying areas) decorated hog-backed tombstones (based on the house-shaped shrines and shrine-tombs reasonably common throughout western Europe in the eighth century and onwards) had probably been introduced from Scotland, and are the only late Scandinavian carved monuments to be placed directly over graves. Strangely they do not occur in the Isle of Man, presumably because of the difficulty of carving the shallow-bedded Manx mudstone three-dimensionally.

Recumbent cross-decorated stones are found *in situ* in a number of cases in the Western Isles, as at Iona, where one stone in particular is related by its runic inscription to the Isle of Man, but no recumbent decorated stones have been recorded in the Isle of Man until well on into the Middle Ages. The upright grave-markers with linear scratched crosses from the Isle of Man, (above, p.48), may be of any date but should be mentioned in this context. Few, if any, have been found in their original position, but their pointed form indicates that they were placed upright in the ground as grave-markers at various unrecorded dates.

The first and perhaps the only surviving late medieval tombstone found in the Island is reputed to be that of Óláfr II, the penultimate Scandinavian king of Man, who died at Rushen Abbey in 1265. This heavy recumbent stone is decorated in relief with a long medieval broadsword like those seen on tombstones in the Western Isles of Scotland. It has no inscription; nevertheless it seems inherently likely that it marked a royal grave. Rushen Abbey, a small, but comparatively rich, Savignac (later Cistercian) monastery, was founded by Óláfr I in 1134, close to the site of an earlier burial ground. By this time the power of the ancient monastic foundations of Western and Northumbrian origin, like Maughold, had dwindled to nothing, and Rushen Abbey was based on an English mother house, Furness in Cumbria. The Abbey was thoroughly plundered by the third earl of Derby, the Lord of Man, as part of the general dissolution of the English monasteries and survives in a ruinous condition today. No site in the Island, however, more clearly demonstrates the growing power of the organised Roman church and of the authority of the medieval bishop of Sodor than his cathedral on St Patrick's Isle, the ruins of which still stand, roofless, to demonstrate the presence of a major medieval ecclesiastical establishment.

CHAPTER 6

The Scandinavian
runic inscriptions

THE INSCRIPTIONS carved on the Manx memorial stones provide a great deal of information concerning the religious, political and social structure of the Isle of Man in the early medieval period. This is particularly true of the Scandinavian runic inscriptions of the tenth and eleventh century which have been briefly considered in the previous chapter. In this chapter the evidence provided by these inscriptions will be examined more closely, as it provides significant clues to the ethnicity and structure of the population of the Island in the period immediately after the Scandinavian settlement. Two earlier stones with Anglo-Saxon runic inscriptions which appear on memorial crosses from Maughold (42 and 43) record the name of an Englishman, *Blagcmon*, have been discussed in an earlier chapter (p. 35), and need not concern us here. For a detailed study and readings of the runes readers should see the forthcoming catalogue of them by Barnes and Knirk referred to in the bibliography.

What are runes?

Runes to many people seem mysterious. In popular imagination they are connected with magic, secrets and gothic horror tales. Although they may occasionally have been used for magical, religious and mysterious purposes, they were in reality perfectly ordinary letters, equivalent to the roman script, and were widely used throughout the Germanic-speaking areas of Europe from the beginning of the first millennium AD. One Manx inscription, however (Andreas 111; fig. 58), is composed of undecipherable runes, denominated as 'cryptic runes', equivalent perhaps to 'codes' intended to be read by a select group of people only.

The individual characters of the runic alphabet are generally made up of straight lines – a vertical stem and one or more 'twigs' set at an angle to the stem; a few characters, however, ʀ (r) and þ (for th), for example, have curved extensions to the stem. The angularity of their form suggests that

Fig. 58. Andreas 111. Cryptic runes in the fragment of side panel of a cross-shaft. Height: 56cm.

they were primarily used on wooden objects by cutting across the grain with a sharp knife (the universal tool carried, mostly by men, on their belt for everyday use). Runes were also cut with a knife or other sharp instrument on objects made of metal, ivory or bone. Indeed, most of the earliest runes (chiefly from Denmark and Schleswig) are cut on the shafts or blades of weapons, mounts, brooches or tools (the earliest examples, from Illerup in Denmark, are dated *c*.200 AD). In England some of the earliest Anglo-Saxon runic inscriptions occur on fifth-century burial-urns from East Anglia. Runic inscriptions first appear on stone monuments in Norway, as at Tune *c*.400; in Sweden, on the side of a stone cist from Kylver, Gotland, in the late fifth century, or, more famously, on a memorial stone from Möjbro, Uppland, dated *c*.500, which carries the incised image of a warrior. They also occur in Anglo-Saxon manuscripts and on Frisian and Anglo-Saxon silver coins. They continued in use in Scandinavia into the medieval period and even later.

Wooden objects inscribed with runes have chiefly survived in waterlogged contexts and have only rarely been found outside Scandinavia. They have been excavated, for example, at the Scandinavian trading port of Hedeby in south Jutland, which in its later phases is contemporary with the Scandinavian settlement of the Isle of Man. At a later period (twelfth to fifteenth century) wooden objects were found in substantial numbers (estimated at 550) in the harbour excavations of the 1950s and '60s at the great mercantile centre of Bergen in Norway. They include merchants' tags which record owners of goods as well as short messages concerning commercial transactions. A few inscriptions have some literary merit, as for example an occasional verse of skaldic character. Other texts are of a social nature – informal messages, even inscrip-

tions of sexually explicit joking character, and a number of personal messages, referring, for example, to love or to the death of a person, or to a
story of trouble with authority. Such inscriptions are not unique to Bergen,
but the number found caused a revolution in understanding of the use of
runes as a script.

Excavation on waterlogged or partly waterlogged sites elsewhere in
Scandinavia has, in the light of the Bergen finds, led to closer examination
of pieces of wood, and has produced similar texts elsewhere. Other inscriptions from all periods are to be found on objects made of bone, walrus ivory
and metal, sometimes indicating ownership, sometimes recording the
name of the craftsman who made an artefact. There are also a number of
casual graffiti.

Where and how were they used?

By the early tenth century, when it first appears in the Isle of Man, the
runic alphabet, the *fuþark*, had evolved in its Scandinavian homeland, from
twenty-four to sixteen characters (fig. 59). The word *fuþark* is formed from
the first six letters of the total rune-row, the whole of which often appears
inscribed as an epigraphic exercise (as in the lowest line of runes on
Maughold 145; fig. 62). Most of the tenth- and eleventh-century runic
inscriptions are carved in stone, sometimes into the living rock (cf. fig. 46).
In Sweden there are some 2,600 such inscriptions, in Denmark about 220,
and in Norway about sixty. It is important to note that these figures do not
include inscriptions on objects made of material other than stone.

About thirty-five runic inscriptions of the period of Scandinavian settlement survive in the Isle of Man (see Appendix, p.151ff), all of which are
carved on stone slabs, All, save two (Maughold 144 and 145), occur on
memorials and are probably grave-markers. In both language and form
they are most closely related to inscriptions found in south-west Norway,
and demonstrate a possible original (if not immediate) home of the Manx
rune-carvers. The total of thirty-five stones found in the Isle of Man compares with only seven texts from stones in Scandinavian runes from
Shetland, six from Orkney, five from western Scotland, and three or four
from England. Most of these comprise texts on memorial stones only
(many of which are fragmentary). Other inscriptions appear on loose
objects, on a comb, and brooches, for example, and on a Romanesque font.
They also appear occasionally as casual graffiti, for example, in a rock-shel-
ter on Holy Island off the east coast of Arran, in Carlisle Cathedral, and in
rather more organised form as a series of twelfth-century inscriptions

incised on the stone lining of a Neolithic chamber-tomb at Maeshowe in Orkney, which was used by Scandinavian travellers as a shelter.

It is to be emphasised that no memorial inscriptions like those found in the Isle of Man occur in the lands around the Irish Sea – neither do any occur on memorial stones in north-west England or in south-west mainland Scotland. The Manx inscriptions thus provide a significant statistical sample, although it must be emphasised and borne in mind that many of the Manx runic texts are fragmentary and some are much worn. They are, however, if sometimes rather rough in grammar and spelling, closely related to runes found in Norway, whence they must have come.

All the runic inscriptions found in the Island, with the exception of the two stones from Maughold cited above, commemorate the dead. The same is largely true in Scandinavia. One great boulder, from Jelling, Denmark, records the achievements of a king, Harald, who raised the stone in memory of 'Gorm his father and Thyre his mother', but also boasts that Harald 'won the whole of Denmark for himself, and Norway and made the Danes Christian'. Harald's father, Gorm, had himself raised a stone in memory of his wife, Thyre, 'Denmark's adornment'. Another stone from Kuli, Norway, was raised in memory of Ulfljótr, 'twelve winters after Christianity had been established in Norway'. Some stones, mainly, but not exclusively, Swedish, record bridge-building or good works, property ownership or other texts of semi-legal import; some are raised by women or commemorate women. Others tell of the death of men in foreign lands as far away as Russia or the west of England, some of whom, it is recorded, served as followers of named Scandinavian chieftains or kings.

Manx runic inscriptions

The Manx rune carvers used the sixteen-stave *fuþark*, known as 'short-twig runes' (*kortkvistruner*).

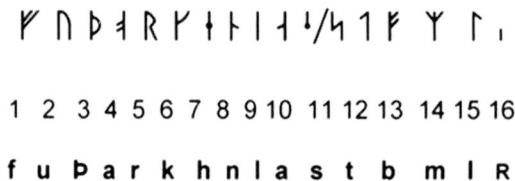

ᚠ ᚢ ᚦ ᚨ ᚱ ᚴ ᚼ ᚾ ᛁ ᛅ ⅟ᚼ ᛏ ᛒ ᛉ ᛚ ᛁ

1 2 3 4 5 6 7 8 9 10 11 12 13 14 15 16

f u þ a r k h n l a s t b m l R

Fig. 59. A 'normal' Manx fuþark. Some inscriptions have additional or modified characters. Transliterated runic characters are conventionally printed in a bold type-face.

Fig. 60. Braddan 138. Part of a runic inscription which reads from bottom left:
(n) r ã s k i t i l : u i l t i : i : t r i k u : a i þ s ã a r a : s i i n
['Hrossketill betrayed his sworn friend in a truce']. Height: 39cm.

This is the type of rune used in Norway and to some extent, particularly in the eleventh century, in Sweden. The form was used less frequently in Denmark. Most Manx runes were cut with a sharp tool to produce a v-shaped incision and are carved along the narrow edge of a cross-slab, starting from bottom left (in one case from the top downwards). In some cases the rune-carver ran out of space and the inscription was carried over onto the face of the stone (as on Kirk Michael 101, see below). In a few cases a substantial portion of the inscription is written on one face of a stone, as on Braddan 138 (fig. 60). On Kirk Michael 130 it appears on the otherwise unornamented face of a cross in two bordering ribbons on either edge, starting at the bottom of the ribbon on the right-hand side, and continuing from the bottom of the shorter ribbon on the left-hand side. On other stones, Ballaugh 106 for example, the inscription runs up a side panel of a main face (fig. 33). Punctuation is provided in various ways by word-

dividers or by dividers of syntactically linked groups of words; occasionally, however, there are no dividers. These dividers consist of a single median point, or a 'colon', either made up of short vertical dashes or cone-
shaped borings. The beginnings and ends of inscriptions are often indicated by a linear cross, either **+** or **x**. In one case (Braddan 135) the inscription terminates in five rather less confidently carved roman letters IHSVS
(Jesus). The best parallels to layout and punctuation are to be found in
western Norway, which is considered to be the homeland of the Manx
runes.

Manx inscriptions, like inscriptions throughout the Scandinavian world
in the tenth and eleventh century, generally record in formulaic terms the
bare details of the person commemorated: 'X raised this stone/cross in
memory of Y, son of Z'. But others are more interesting, recording, for
example, the name of the rune-carver or making short deferential or pious
statements. Close study of a name often reveals hidden significances, indicating, for example, a person's ethnic origin and his or her relationship to
members of such communities. Detailed analysis of the content of the
inscriptions sometimes enables us to broaden our knowledge of the Scandinavian settlement considerably.

One example gives an idea of the way in which a straightforward inscription may be mined for internal information: Kirk Michael 101 (fig. 32) has
an inscription along one edge, which spills over onto one face, and reads:

> **xmail:brikti:sunr:aþakans:smiþ:raisti:kross:_anã:fur:salu:**
> **sina: sin brukuin:kaut x kirþi: þ̣ạnã:auk | ala: imaun x**
> Malbrigþi son of Áedhacán the smith raised this cross for his soul
> … but Gautr made this and all in Man.

An incidental, but important, piece of information provided by this
inscription is the word **maun**, the first written record on the Island of its
name, and probably the earliest incontrovertible contemporary mention of
the Isle of Man in any source (see above p.4). But the inscription is important for many other reasons.

It tells that the man (for only men are recorded as raising crosses in the
Island) who paid for the cross had a name, *Malbrigþi*, which implies that he
was a follower (or servant) of the early Irish saint Bridget. His Gaelic name
thus indicates his adherence to Christianity, emphasised by the fact that he
memorialised his father by raising a cross in his memory. Whether this was
his original given name or one given on conversion is not clarified, but the
fact that his father had a Gaelic name, Áedhacán, suggests that Malbrigþi

was either a second-generation convert to Christianity, or a native of the Island or another Celtic-speaking country. Áedhacán is described as a smith, probably a blacksmith, a craftsman of high importance in the Scandinavian world as the weapons he made could be responsible for a man's life and death. Smiths would often have had free status and could have been wealthy. Such wealth and status is indicated by the inscription on a stone at Hørning in Denmark, 'Toke the smith raised this stone in memory of Thorgisl, Gudmund's son, who gave him gold and freedom'. It is entirely possible that the father and son named on the Kirk Michael cross came from a native stock and that the profession of the father was such that, as a smith, he was valued by the settlers and retained his status as a freeman.

The carver of the stone was a man with a Scandinavian name, Gautr, who boasted that he 'made this [cross] and all in Man'. Whether this was an advertisement or whether it was indeed an accurate statement cannot be determined. Accurate or not, Gautr might indeed have been the first person to have carved runes in the Island, for one ornamental element on this cross is executed in a true version of the Borre style's ring-chain, stylistically the earliest Scandinavian motif used in the Island. He is also named on another stone, Andreas 99, which states that he came from **kuli**, a place-name which has been associated with the Hebridean island of Coll, but might also be a local Manx place-name (e.g. Cooil, although this name is only first recorded in the eighteenth century). The Andreas stone bears a slightly more developed version of the Borre ring-chain and may be marginally later than the Kirk Michael cross – the product of a more mature Gautr?

It is, then, entirely possible that the commissioner of the Kirk Michael cross was a native Celt. His father, a man with a Gaelic name, almost certainly was. But this begs the question as to why the stone is decorated with a Scandinavian motif and has a Norse inscription. The most reasonable hypothesis is that the stone followed the native tradition of stone carving and was simply fashionable, and that the Scandinavian Gautr had learned a new trade in order to carve the cross in a fashion which was related to earlier local memorial stones carved in a native tradition. The ornament of the Kirk Michael stone was derived in part from other media in Norway, in part from England and in part from the Island, while the form of the cross-slab was certainly Manx. An innovation was the use of a memorial inscription in runes and in the language of the Scandinavian settlers.

Only one other named sculptor is recorded on a Manx cross-slab, an

eleventh-century man named Arni carved the inscription of Maughold 142.
He signed it with the formula **arni:risti:runar:þisar**, using the verb *rista*
(to carve), which, while common in Denmark and Sweden, does not
appear in Norway until the late tenth century – and then very rarely. He
probably also carved the crosses on the stone, and even, possibly, the representation of a ship with furled sails (see above p.121). Gautr, however,
used the word *karþi*, which also means 'carved', but is of earlier date.
Gautr's two statements, however, probably imply that he carved the whole
stone and not just the inscription (below p.134). On Onchan 141, however, a woman called *Þúriþ* wrote some runes (probably a graffito), using a
variant of Arni's formula, but perhaps not all the scattered inscriptions on
the stone (below p.138).

The names of the three craftsmen (two sculptors/rune-carvers and a
smith) discussed above all belong to the period of Scandinavian settlement
and conversion. The name, Juan/John, on two stones (Maughold 145; fig.
62, and 144), which are not memorials, is that of a twelfth-century priest,
from a period when Christianity was well established and when historiated
crosses had ceased to be produced.

The content of the inscriptions

One of the most complete of the Manx runic inscriptions is Kirk Michael
no. 130:

> : mal : lümkun raisti : kross : þïna : ïftïr : mal : murü :
> fustra : sinï : tätãrtufkals : kãna: is : aþisl : ati + //]ïtra :
> ïs : laifa fustra ku : kuþan : þan : sãn : ilan +
>
> Mallymkun raised this cross in memory of Malmury, his foster
> [father/mother], Dufgal's daughter, the wife whom Aþísl owned
> [i.e.was married to]. Better to leave a good foster than a bad son.

It is unusual physically as it is placed in a ribbon with the inscription
starting bottom right and continuing bottom left (the break indicated by
the forward slashes).

First, the names: three, *Mallymkun*, *Malmury* and *Dufgal*, are Gaelic (presumably Irish); *Aþísl* is Norse. The genders of the first two could be of
either sex, but as Mallymkun is the commissioner, the probability that the
name is masculine is supported by the following noun **fustra**, which is
masculine; further it it should be noted that only men seem to have erected memorials in the Island. Malmury, however, could be the name either
of a man or of a woman. The grammar is difficult and has been much dis-

cussed by philologists. The weight of philological opinion is that the name Malmury (servant of Mary) is female. The two first names imply that their bearers were Christian, as was Malbrigþi (the servant of St Bridget) on Kirk Michael 101. The two names on Kirk Michael 130 mean 'the servant of Lymkun' and 'the servant of Mary', the latter presumably referring to the Virgin. Attempts have been made to identify 'Lymkun', with an early Irish follower of St Patrick, *Lomchiu*, but this suggestion has not been received with wild enthusiasm. The origin of the names illustrates the conversion to Christianity of Scandinavian settlers, and perhaps also intermarriage between the settlers and the settled – a common enough feature on crosses raised in the Island during the conversion period. The last clause of this inscription makes a statement about the memorialised person and is perhaps using the words of an existing proverb, or is referring to the man who raised the cross. Such throw-away lines are rare, but not unknown, on the Manx crosses.

A more 'in-your-face' statement is contained in the now incomplete inscription on one side of the fragment of the head of a cross from Braddan (138; fig. 60), It records that 'Hrossketill betrayed his sworn friend in a truce [**i tryggu**]'. It is a pity that the rest of the inscription on this stone is missing as it would have been interesting to know whether this is the name of the dead man or of his betrayer. The latter is unlikely unless the relatives of the dead man wanted to advertise his guilt, which would be the case if there was a missing word, 'but', at the beginning of the inscription. The inscription is unusual as, uniquely for the Island, it started on the (mostly missing) shaft of the cross and continued across the bar of the cross to end in a ribbon on the right-hand side of the cross-head. There are parallels to the record of betrayal on memorial stones in other parts of the Scandinavian world. For example, a twelfth-century runic memorial stone from Nora, Uppland, Sweden, records the death of a man in what seems to have been a quarrel about a family estate some 30km away. Another very fine Swedish stone from Sjonhem on Gotland records the death of three sons in Romania (in Wallachia), where they were betrayed by the locals.

Bearing in mind that many of the Manx stones are merely fragments, there are according to Judith Jesch forty-eight personal names on the surviving stones. Nine Gaelic names are masculine and three are feminine. Twenty-four Norse names are masculine and five are feminine. The four names recorded in the twelfth century by Juan/John the priest (including his own) on Maughold 144 and 145 – all masculine Gaelic – are the prod-

uct of a learned priest, and include three saints' names, but do not belong
to the main series of memorial stones. Three stones (as has been shown)
record the name of the sculptor (one of whom also records his father's
name), while another (a woman's name) is possibly a graffito. None of the
people recorded as having commissioned stones are women, but four wives
(plus one unnamed), two foster-mothers and one daughter are named on
the stones. Eight commemorate men (two of whom are fathers). Three
sons are mentioned; the stone also records the uncle of the commemorated man. One man commemorated himself, while the relationships of two
others do not survive. Two nicknames, *Sandulfr the Black* and *Þorulfr the
Red*, presumably refer to the colour of their hair. Another nickname has
defied attempts at translation or interpretation, *Þorleifr hnakki* on Braddan
135.

Let us return to the names of the carvers recorded on the three stones
named above. One, Maughold 142, clearly states that the runes were
carved by Arni (**arni risti runar þisar**). But Gautr, on Andreas 99 and
Kirk Michael 101, does not say that he was the rune-writer, rather on both
his crosses he uses the word 'carved' (*karþi*), but does not say what he
'carved'. It is likely that he was both sculptor and rune-writer, as *karþi* is
singular. Unfortunately desperate attempts to recognise the same hand on
the two stones have reached no conclusion. On the other hand the personal details Gautr gives on his two stones suggest that he was, as Terje
Spurkland has pointed out, an important man, who was proud to claim
that he had carved the runes on both crosses and 'all in Man'. Indeed, the
ornament on both stones in all its simplicity and discipline could also have
been done by the same hand, an argument strengthened by the fact that
neither stone carried representations of animals or other figures. There is
an increasing realisation – triggered by the recognition of the large number
of incidental runic inscriptions on the Bergen finds – that runes were read
and carved by many classes of people and were in daily use. It should also
be apparent that the presence of a large number of memorial inscriptions
throughout the Scandinavian world must have been intended to be read by
literate people.

There were undoubtedly professional rune-masters in Scandinavia at this
period. In eleventh-century central Sweden a number of craftsmen seem to
have dominated the production of runic inscriptions, and their names are
recorded on many of the large number of Swedish rune-stones. Indeed, on
a few stones it is clearly stated that the man who carved the runes was different from the man who carved the stones, while on one stone, from

Gerstaberg in Södermanland, it is stated that 'Äsbjörn cut and Ulv painted' [the stone]; but it is also clear that many of the people who carved the stones also carved the inscriptions. Such must have been the case in the Isle of Man, although attempts to identify particular hands on the Manx crosses have so far run into the ground.

Chronology and identity

There is little that can be said about the language of the Manx memorial crosses, save that some are more grammatically correct than others. It is significant that, apart from some of the personal names, the Manx inscriptions are written in West Norse. There are, however, occasional Danish traits, which might have crept in from the English settlements. Only one word has a Gaelic root, the word for 'cross' (*kross*), which occurs twelve times (it also occurs twice in the slender corpus of crosses in the Northern and Western Isles of Scotland and once in the even more slender corpus of runic inscriptions in Ireland). Strangely the word also appears on a stone from Sockburn, Co. Durham. The word may be indicative of the early arrival of Christianity among the Scandinavian settlers of the Island. In pagan Norway crosses were not yet being raised, and the word would have had no significance in a pre-Christian community. In Sweden, where the inscriptions are generally of eleventh-century date, there are no memorial stones of the type found in the Island, although inscribed crosses occasionally occur on the face of a stone. In Denmark, where runic inscriptions of similar date to the Manx examples are found, the inscriptions are placed on stones, many of which are boulders, so that variations of the word *kumbl* for 'monument' or *stain* for 'stone' are used.

It is noteworthy that the runes on the cross from Inchmarnock, Bute, are very similar epigraphically to those, for example, on the cross-head Braddan 138 and, as on the Manx example, the text emerges from the shaft to continue outside the head of a cross. The date of the Inchmarnock stone, incidentally, has been suggested as 'after *c*.1000', on the basis of the letter **ï** in the word *þïni*, which is a modified letter that also appears on Kirk Michael 130.

The verb *setti* ('placed/set') on Maughold 142 is important in that it replaces the normal word used in the Island for erecting a stone, which was *reisti* (raised). This is a common replacement in Danish and Swedish inscriptions after *c*.1000, but is very rare in Norway. It supports the argument (above p.121) that this is perhaps one of the latest stones in the Manx corpus, and would tend to indicate a date for this stone near the end of the tenth century. But caution may be necessary as the runes, including the *fuþark*, carved by the priest Juan/John on Maughold 144 and 145, are of the normal tenth-century type, while the stones have been dated after 1148, if the name *Malachi* which appears on this stone refers to the archbishop of Armagh who died in that year.

Perhaps one of the most extraordinary features of the Manx crosses is that there are no directly Christian invocations of the kind found on Scandinavian memorial stones. Variants of the phrase 'may God help his soul' are found frequently on early eleventh-century stones in Sweden and at least once in Norway, but in Denmark although there are only five examples, they are generally earlier. There is, however, one stone in the Island, Kirk Michael 101 (see above) where 'Malbrigþi, son of Áedhacán…raised this cross for his soul… (**raisti : kross : þanã : fur : salu : sina**). This is the earliest record of the word *salu* in a Scandinavian language (a loan word from English).

The name of God does not appear in any of the Manx runic inscriptions, but Christ's name was read by both Kermode and Page as IHSVS at the end of the runic inscription on Braddan 135, under the head of the cross. The first three letters are a contraction of Christ's name, although the letters 'V' and 'S', which seem to be read correctly, are difficult to interpret. The only other reference to Christ is the inscription in runes which appears on the presently unseen back of Onchan 141, which may be a graffito (see below). It is inscribed in two lines; within the cross-head is: **x isukrist** (*Jesus Christ*) and, above the head of the cross, the single word, **kru[** (cross). Christ's name also appears on the much later stone Maughold 144.

This reluctance to refer to Christ is mirrored by the sparsity of the images of Christ which appear on the crosses carved in the Scandinavian period (see above p.112). He appears, crucified, on the Calf of Man crucifix (Rushen 61; fig. 51), which is for the Island *sui generis*, but is based on images freely found in Ireland (above p.110).

Onchan 141 – a case study

This stone (fig. 61) is atypical and deserves special attention. Each face is provided with an unembellished ring-headed cross, one of which has a shaft longer than that on the other face. If the crosses are plain, the inscriptions are a muddle, although on one face they are reasonably normal and, in part, can be interpreted. On the face with the longer shaft is an inscription set in two rows to the left of the shaft; this reads from the bottom left

Fig. 61. Onchan 141. Height: 114cm.

corner, turning at the top of the shaft and continuing down to the (broken) base of the stone. On the right-hand side of the shaft the inscription continues to the top (the question-marks indicate doubtful letters and the vertical strokes the start of a new ribbon):

]sunr x raisti x ift?u?nusina | murkialu x m x | ukikat x aukraþir?t

...son raised after his wife murkialu ...

While the first two rows have been reasonably translated, the first row on the other side of the shaft of the cross (the outer row is damaged and incomplete, and the staves are casually placed) was the subject of particularly close study by the Norwegian runologist Magnus Olsen in 1911. His analysis of the inscription is complicated, but he read the third row as 'I think about them [i.e. the runes] and interpret them properly'. His argument has been widely, but rarely enthusiastically, accepted.

The inscriptions on the other face of the stone have not been seen for years as the stone is mounted against the wall, but drawings by Kermode exist. They are presumably, like all his drawings, reasonably accurate and have been used by all students in recent years. The two inscriptions are placed at the base of the cross and read:

| **þuriþ x raist x runï** | and | **x isukrist** | **kru[** |
| þúríþ wrote the runes | | Jesus Christ | cross |

Which seem clear enough.

The female name *Þúríþ* is of great interest as it is the only known example of a woman as a carver of an inscription on stone. As noted above, it has been suggested that this particular inscription is a graffito, one of many of various dates on Manx stones, but, if so, it was carved in a very confident hand, unlike most of the others. There is no inherent reason why a woman should not have carved a main inscription on the stone. However, in Sweden, where there are very many recorded names of rune-masters on stone memorials, not a single woman's name has been found, although a stone from Jättendal, Hälsingland, records that a woman, Gunnborga, 'coloured the stone'. At least one woman has been noticed as a carver on bone; a rejected lover, Sigvor, cursed a man, Ingemar, in a graffito on a bone weaving-tablet from Lund in Sweden (at that time part of Denmark). The Onchan stone provides evidence of a woman's literacy in the Isle of Man at this period, but then the fact that there are so many crosses bearing runic inscriptions in the Island would imply that there were a number of people who were rune-literate, even if we have no evidence here, as we have in Scandinavia, of a woman commissioning a memorial.

'Irish Sea runes'

There is some evidence that runes like those used in the Isle of Man were used more generally in the region. Two large pieces of silver bullion of late ninth- or early tenth-century date carry runic inscriptions which are often compared to the Manx runes. One comes from a hoard from Flusco Pike,

Fig. 62. Maughold 145. A runic inscription by Juan/John, 'priest in Cornadali' (Cornaa). Below is a reasonably accurate ogam alphabet. Height: 33cm.

near Penrith in Cumbria, and is lightly, but neatly, scratched on the hoop of a silver bossed penannular brooch with an incomplete *fuþark*; these are runes of a type, according to Barnes and Page, found only in the Isle of Man. The hoard was probably deposited in the first quarter of the tenth century, perhaps by Scandinavian settlers who had contact with some of the first settlers in Man. Perhaps more interesting is the well-known and splendid Hiberno-Saxon pseudo-penannular brooch from Hunterston, West Kilbride, now in the National Museums of Scotland. It is dated to the seventh or eighth century, but was so grand that it could have been in use until the ninth century, when this type of brooch went out of fashion. On the back of the hoop is a scratched inscription which reads: **mal-briþaastilk**. The first eight letters, **malbriþa**, is presumably the same name as that on Kirk Michael 101, meaning 'servant of Bridget' (see above p.133), while the element **stilk** may be a byname, hence 'Melbrigþi stilk [owns me]'. Barnes and Page write that such runes are 'used on many of the Manx rune stones'. The runes were presumably added to the brooch in the early tenth century by the then owner in the Irish Sea region. The brooches from Flusco Pike and Hunterston are the only two secular objects on which the 'Manx' runic script is used, although they were probably not made in the Island.

A footnote

Practically invisible on one face of a cross from Kirk Michael (130) are two ogam inscriptions. On the elaborately-ornamented face of the cross, below the main decoration, is a competently executed attempt to incise the ogam alphabet of twenty characters (fig. 63 left). On the other face, between the two elements of the long runic inscription, is a worn ogam inscription (fig. 63 right) which has defied interpretation. They were already recorded in the nineteenth century and later illustrated in a line drawing by Kermode (fig. 63). On Maughold 145 (fig. 62), one of two stones found in the parish of Maughold, is an inscription by a twelfth-century priest, Juan/John, in runic characters (see above p.132), who also carved the inscription on 144. Below it is inscribed part of a well-formed and accurate ogam alphabet. This is written in late (sometimes labelled 'scholastic') ogams, as is a very rough inscription on a stone excavated by *Time Team* at the burial-ground at Speke in Braddan (no. 189).

Such stones beg an interesting question: was the ogam script used by the priests in the indigenous tradition after the Scandinavian settlement?

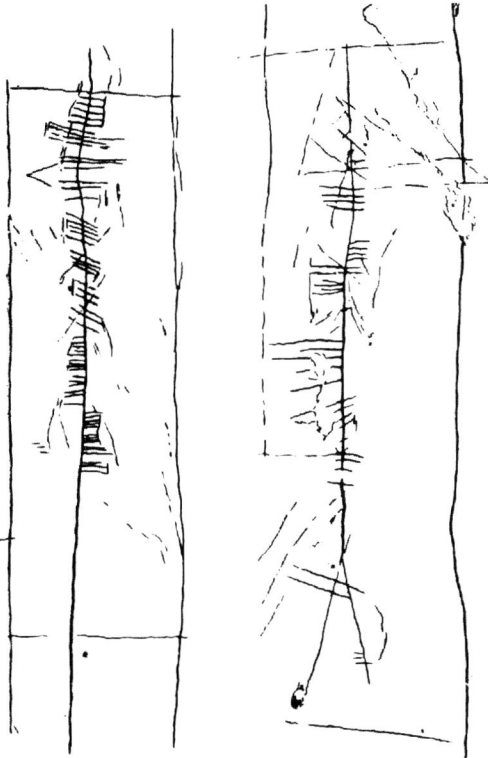

Fig. 63. Drawings by P. M. C. Kermode of ogam inscriptions on Kirk Michael 130. To the left is a version of the ogam alphabet; to the right is an unintelligible series of strokes which presumably imitate the ogam alphabet.

BIBLIOGRAPHY & SUGGESTED READING

THIS IS A BOOK for the general reader as detailed references in footnotes and endnotes can be off-putting, especially as much of the literature is in a variety of languages. In the annotated list below there are suggestions for further reading on the main themes. As the book will, I hope, also be used by students on the borderline of the subject, I have provided a rather more detailed commentary than is strictly necessary for a general audience.

Abbreviations

Fell (1983). C. Fell et al. (eds.), *The Viking Age in the Isle of Man. Select papers from the ninth Viking Congress, Isle of Man 4-14 July 1981* (London 1983).

Freke (2002). D. Freke, *Excavations on St Patrick's Isle, Peel, Isle of Man 1982-88. Prehistoric, Viking, Medieval and later* (Liverpool 2002). Centre for Manx Studies Monographs 2.

JMM. Journal of the Manx Museum.

MAS. The Manx Archaeological Survey, parts 1-5, 1909-18. Reissued as a single volume with part 6, 1966, as two volumes (Douglas 1968).

NHM. A New History of the Isle of Man, (Liverpool 2000-).

TIMNHAS. Transactions/Proceedings of the Isle of Man Natural History and Antiquarian Society.

Wilson (2008). D. M. Wilson, *The Vikings in the Isle of Man* (Aarhus 2008).

The background

The indispensable study of the sculpture is P. M. C. Kermode's *Manx Crosses* (London 1904). More useful is the second edition (Balgavies, 1994), as it reprints articles he published recording new finds up until 1929. By using this edition the reader is able to see illustrations of all the stones, including many minor stones not reproduced in this book. It also contains a list of all relevant work published by Kermode and later scholars. Further references to illustrations published since that date will be found in the Appendix (p.151ff). An important later study is an unpublished Ph.D thesis by Ross Trench-Jellicoe, *A re-definition and stylistic analysis of P. M. C. Kermode's pre-Scandinavian series of Manx sculptured monuments* (University of Lancaster, 1985), which has a remarkable bibliography, but concentrates mainly on stones produced before the tenth century.

Important comparative material will be found in the corpus of Scottish stones by J. Romilly Allen and Joseph Anderson, *The early Christian monuments of Scotland*, two volumes, London 1903. It was republished in 1993 (Balgavies). See also the latest interpretations of the Scottish stones by George and Isabel Henderson, *The art of the Picts. Sculpture and metalwork in early medieval Scotland* (London 2004), and Ian Fisher's corpus of the *Early medieval sculpture in the West Highlands and Islands* (Edinburgh 2001), which are important, as is Derek Craig's 'Pre-Norman sculpture in Galloway; a review of the evidence', in R. D. Oram and G. P. Stell, *Galloway: land and lordship* (Edinburgh 1991), 45-62. Unfortunately no complete corpus of Irish sculpture exists, but readers will find Françoise Henry's *La sculpture irlandaise pendant les deux premiers siècles de l'ère chrétienne* (Paris 1932) useful, if they can find it! Otherwise, a combination of the same author's three-volume work *Irish Art* (London 1965-70), P. Harbison's *The High Crosses of Ireland, an iconographical and photographic survey* (1992, Bonn, Römisch-Germanisches Zentralmuseum; Forschungsinstitut für Vor- und Frühgeschichte: Monographien 17.1), and P. Lionard's 'Early Irish crosses', in *Proceedings of the Royal Irish Academy*, 61, Section C, no. 5, 1961, 95-169, give a good conspectus of the Irish material. The British Academy's *Corpus of Anglo-Saxon Stone Sculpture* (Oxford 1984-), which will be completed within the next few years, is also indispensable, as is *A corpus of medieval inscribed stones and stone sculpture in Wales* (University of Wales Press 2007-2013).

For the general background to the Isle of Man in the period of the sculpture (c.500-1040), *The Manx Archaeological Survey (MAS)* is the only survey of burial-grounds (although out of date in respect of the keeills). C. D. Morris's publication of the excavation of a burial ground at Keeill Vael is the only modern report on such a site, in Fell 1983, *The Viking Age in the Isle of Man. Select papers from the ninth Viking Congress, Isle of Man 4-14 July 1981* (London 1983). Freke 2002 contains much information from this multi-period site – a royal fortification and the seat of the diocese of Sodor and Man – and is very useful. Less useful, but important, is the report on another multi-period site, G. J. H. Neely, 'Excavations at Ronaldsway, Isle of Man', *Antiquaries Journal*, 20 (1940), 22-86. Otherwise, keen students will look at the *Transactions/Proceedings of the Isle of Man Natural History and Antiquarian Society (TIMNHAS)* in its various guises since 1879, and the many short papers in the *Journal of the Manx Museum* (1924-80, *JMM*). The second volume of *A new history of the Isle of Man* (Liverpool University Press) should appear shortly and includes various chapters on this period with a full critical apparatus. D. M. Wilson, 'Conversion and Christian symbolism in the Isle of Man', *TIMNHAS*, 12:4, (2014), 573-95, summarises the two periods of conversion to Christianity.

General histories of the lands around the Irish Sea abound. John Blair's *The church in Anglo-Saxon Society* (Oxford 2005), brings a breath of fresh air to the subject, as does T. M. Charles-Edwards' *Early Christian Ireland* (Cambridge 2000). Edel Bhreathnach's *Ireland in the medieval world, landscape, kingship and religion* (Dublin 2014) is a more popular account of the subject. See also James Campbell, *Essays in Anglo-Saxon history* (London 1986). Wendy Davies, *Wales in the early Middle Ages* (Leicester 1982) is important. Scotland is less easy. Alex Woolf, *From Pictland to Alba 789-1070* (Edinburgh 2007) is useful, but does not cover the whole period. Sally M. Foster, *Picts, Gaels and Scots* (London 1996) is a lively introduction to the subject.

Introduction

A useful introduction to the early study of the Viking Age in England is in R. I. Page, 'Some thoughts on Manx Runes', *Saga-Book of the Viking Society*, 20, 1980, 179-99 (re-printed in R. I. Page, *Runes and runic inscriptions. Collected essays on Anglo-Saxon and Viking runes* (Woodbridge 1995), 161-80). For terminology of the word 'Celtic' see W. Davies, 'The myth of the Celtic Church', in N. Edwards and A. Lane, *The early Church in Wales and the West. Recent work in early Christian archaeology, history and place-names* (Oxford 1992), 12-21; Oxbow monograph 16. For 'Viking' see C. Fell, 'Modern English *Viking*', *Leeds studies in English*, 18, 11-23 and Judith Jesch, *The Viking diaspora* (Oxford 2015), 4-10. For the latter-day life of the ornament on the Manx crosses, see E. Wilson, 'Celts, Vikings and Archibald Knox' in *TIMNHAS*, 11:3, (2004), 395-422.

Chapter 1

There is no up-to-date modern history of the Isle of Man before the beginning of the eleventh century, although the second volume of *NHM*, which should shortly appear, deals with this period. The first volume, edited by Richard Chiverell and Geoffrey Thomas, *The evolution of the Manx landscape*

(Liverpool 2006) deals with both solid and economic geology and the period after the Ice Age, including a chapter on the contemporary landscape.

Kathleen Hughes, *Early Christian Ireland: introduction to the sources* (London 1972) provides what it says on the label. Otherwise, the general histories of the lands around the Irish Sea and of the coming of Christianity to Britain, listed above, are among the best interpretations of the sources. See also Ludwig Bieler, 'Ireland's contribution to the Culture of Northumbria in G. Bonner (ed.) *Famulus Christi, Essays in commemoration of the thirteenth centenary of the Venerable Bede* (London 1976), 210-28. K. Hughes, 'Evidence for contacts between the Churches of the Irish and English from the Synod of Whitby to the Viking Age' in *England before the Conquest, Studies in primary sources presented to Dorothy Whitelock* (Cambridge 1971), 49-67, is important. See also C. Stancliffe, *Bede, Wilfrid and the Irish*, Jarrow lecture 2003. Specialists should be aware of *Peritia – Journal of the Medieval Academy of Ireland* (1982-), which contains a vast amount of interpretation of the sources by leading scholars. Charles Thomas's *The early Christian archaeology of North Britain* (Oxford 1971) is still useful.

Chapter 2

For pre-Scandinavian graves we can only rely on the *MAS* and Freke (2002), 58-62, which is the most useful account of a continuous cemetery. A number of lintel graves are published in *TIMNHAS*. See also Morris under the heading 'The background' in Fell (1983). One of the most important pieces of evidence chronologically is the Balladoole site – G. Bersu and J. R. Bruce, 'A prehistoric early Christian and Viking site at Balladoole, Kirk Arbory, Isle of Man', *TIMNHAS*, 7:4, (1974), 632-665, and Bersu and Wilson cited below, p.147.

The literature on the earliest inscribed stones in the British Isles is immense; see R. A. S. Macalister, *Corpus inscriptionum insularum celticarum*, vol. 2 (Dublin 1949), and K. Jackson, *Language and history in early Britain* (Edinburgh 1953). P. Sims-Williams, *The Celtic Inscriptions of Britain. Phonology and Chronology c.500-1200* (Oxford 2003). K. Jackson, 1950, 'Notes on the Ogam inscriptions of southern Britain', in C. Fox and B. Dickins (eds.), *The early cultures of north-west Europe (H. M. Chadwick memorial studies)*, (Cambridge 1950), 199-203. For Anglo-Saxon runes, see R. I. Page, *An introduction to English runes*, 2nd. ed. (Woodbridge 1999).

For surveys of keeills, see *MAS*, passim. For St Patrick's Isle see Freke (2002). For the Tynwald Plain see D. M. Wilson and J. Kewley, 'The

Tynwald complex', *TIMNHAS*, 12:4, (2014), 773-786. Keeills, once thought to be chapels of early Christian date, are now generally agreed to date to the tenth century and later. Little has been written on this re-dating, but see discussion and references in Wilson 2008, 18 and passim. See also T. Ó Carragáin, 'Cemetery settlements and local churches in pre-Viking Ireland in light of comparisons with England and Wales', in J. Graham-Campbell, and M. Ryan (eds.), *Anglo-Saxon/Irish relations before the Vikings* (Oxford 2009), Proceedings of the British Academy, 157, 329-66.

Chapter 3

The early pages of *NHM*, vol. 3 (2015) are useful for this chapter. George Broderick's edition of *Chronicles of the Kings of Man and the Isles*, 2nd ed. (Douglas 1996), provides the Latin text and translation of the first exclusively Manx document. For Maughold see B. R. S. Megaw, 'The monastery of St Maughold', *TIMNHAS*, 5:2, (1950), 169-80. For St Patrick's Isle see Freke (2002). For the Dunwich seal see D. M. Wilson, *Anglo-Saxon ornamental metalwork, 700-1100, in the British Museum* (London 1964), 80-1. For St Cuthbert's altar, see C. F. Battiscombe (ed.), *The Relics of St Cuthbert* (Durham 1956), 326-36.

For Whithorn and other Galloway sites see R. G. Collingwood, 'The early crosses of Galloway', *Transactions of the Dumfries and Galloway Natural History and Antiquarian Society*, 3 ser:10, 1922-3, 205-31; D. J. Craig 'Pre-Norman sculpture in Galloway. Some territorial implications' in R. D. Oram and G. P. Stell (eds.), *Galloway. Land and lordship* (Edinburgh 1991). Derek Craig's unpublished PhD thesis, *The distribution of pre-Norman sculpture in South-West Scotland: Provenance, ornament and regional groups* (Durham 1992), is the only modern study of the whole subject. For Hartlepool: R. Daniels, 'The Anglo-Saxon monastery at Hartlepool, England' in J. Hawkes and S. Mills (eds), *Northumbria's golden age* (Stroud 1999), 105-125. For Clonmacnoise, R. A. S. Macalister, *The memorial slabs of Clonmacnois, King's County* (Dublin 1909). For Paul and Anthony see C. M. Thomas, 'Missing models: visual narrative in insular Paul and Anthony panels', in *Making histories. Proceedings of the sixth international conference on insular art* (Donington 2013), 77-89.

Chapter 4

A series of essays concerning Scandinavian activity in ninth and tenth-century Ireland, and important to an understanding of the situation in the

Irish Sea, is H. B. Clarke and R. Johnson (eds.), *The Vikings in Ireland and beyond: before and after the Battle of Clontarf* (Dublin 2015), particularly the articles by E. Purcell, E. P. Keely, G. Williams, C. Etchingham, B. Hodgkinson and the ever-critical D. Ó Corráin. In the same volume Clare Downham, *inter alia*, discusses Scandinavian activity in Galloway. D. Griffiths, *Vikings of the Irish Sea* (Stroud 2010), is a good summary of the region. I. Russell and M. F. Hurley (eds.), *Woodstown: a Viking-Age settlement in Co. Waterford* (Dublin 2014) is important in relation to the precursor of towns outside Dublin. The Dublin excavations are gradually being published by the National Museum of Ireland, but it would be tedious to list all the volumes and series.

A number of papers in J. Graham-Campbell and M. Ryan (eds.), *Anglo-Saxon/Irish relations before the Vikings*, (Oxford 2009), Proceedings of the British Academy, 157, are relevant to this chapter, particularly: F. Edmonds, 'Practicalities of communication between Northumbrian and Irish Churches', 129-57; E. Campbell, 'Anglo-Saxon/Gaelic interaction in Scotland', 253-64; D. M. Wilson, 'Stylistic influences in early Manx sculpture', 311-328, and T. Ó Carragáin, 'Cemetery settlements and local churches in pre-Viking Ireland in light of comparisons with England and Wales', 329-66. For sculpture in the Irish Sea, see R. N. Bailey, 'Irish Sea contacts in the Viking Period', *Beretning fra tredie tværfaglige Vikingesymposium* (Aarhus 1984), 7-36. Papers in H. B. Clarke et al. (eds.), *Ireland and Scandinavia in the early Viking Age* (Dublin 1998) are pertinent, as are contributions to J. Sheehan and D. Ó Corráin (eds.), *The Viking Age: Ireland and the West* (Dublin 2010), Proceedings of the fifteenth Viking Congress. See also D. N. Dumville, *The churches of North Britain in the first Viking Age* (Whithorn 1997), Fifth Whithorn lecture. A. Ritchie (ed.), *Govan and its medieval sculpture* (Stroud 1994), is useful. R. Trench-Jellicoe, 'Manx sculptured stones and the early Viking Age', in P. Davey and D. Finlayson, *Mannin revisited. Twelve essays on Manx culture and environment* (Edinburgh 2002), 11-36.

Caroline Paterson et al., *Shadows in the sand: Excavation of a Viking-Age cemetery at Cumwhitton in Cumbria* (Lancaster 2014), is not only an exemplary excavation report; it also tackles Cumbria's place in the Scandinavian diaspora in the Irish Sea and the Western Isles of Scotland. For graves of the Scandinavian settlements in Ireland, see Stephen H. Harrison and Raghnall Ó Floinn, *Viking graves and grave-goods in Ireland* (Dublin 2014), which gives all the references. See James Graham-Campbell and Colleen E. Batey, *Vikings in Scotland. An archaeological survey* (Edinburgh 1998).

For Norwegian parallels see B. Solberg, 'From paganism to Christianity in Norway – an examination of graves and grave finds', in I. Bang et al. (eds.), *Nordic Middle Ages – artefacts, landscapes and society. Essays in honour of Ingvild Øye on her 70th birthday* (Bergen 2015), University of Bergen Archaeological Series, 62, 75-88. For the Danelaw, see J. Richards, 'The case of the missing Vikings: Scandinavian burial in the Danelaw', in S. Lucy and A. Reynolds (eds.), *Burial in early medieval England and Wales* (London 2002), The Society for medieval archaeology: Monograph Series, no. 17. Articles by various authors in J. R. Baldwin and D. Whyte (eds.), *The Scandinavians in Cumbria* (Edinburgh 1985), are now out of date but the book contains a number of topics not covered elsewhere. S. E. Harding et al. (eds.), *In search of the Vikings, Interdisciplinary approaches to the Scandinavian heritage of North-West England* (Boca Ratan 2015) is what its title implies. For the Isle of Man, see Wilson 2008. G. Bersu and D. M. Wilson, *Three Viking graves in the Isle of Man*, (London 1966), The Society for Medieval Archaeology, Monograph series 1. See also Wilson in Graham-Campbell and Ryan (cited above). See also D. M. Hadley and J. Richards (eds.) *Cultures in Contact: Scandinavian settlement in England in the ninth and tenth centuries* (Turnhout 2000).

C. Etchingham, 'North Wales, Ireland and the Isles: the Insular Viking zone', *Peritia*, 15, 2001, 145-187, is particularly useful for Wales. See also M. Redknap, *Vikings in Wales. An archaeological quest* (Cardiff 2000). Publication of hoards of precious metal, chiefly silver, has received a great deal of attention since Michael Dolley and Christopher Blunt began a rigorous re-examination of the coinage in the 1950s. Their work has been continued by many scholars in Britain and Europe, particularly by Mark Blackburn, see R. Naismith et al. (eds.), *Early medieval numismatic history. Studies in memory of Mark Blackburn* (Fulham 2014). A less weighty work which includes objects of silver, but is a useful for coins as well, is James Graham-Campbell and Gareth Williams (eds.), *Silver economy in the Viking Age* (Walnut Creek 2007). For the objects found in hoards, which has increased almost exponentially in the last half-century due to the activity of metal detectorists, James Graham-Campbell, *The Cuerdale hoard and related Viking-Age silver and gold from Britain and Ireland in the British Museum* (London 2011), British Museum Research Publication, 185, is essential.

Chapter 5

A good popular book on the Viking Age is P. Sawyer (ed.), *The Oxford histo-*

ry of the Vikings (Oxford 1997). More up-to-date and more thorough is S. Brink and N. Price (eds.), *The Viking world* (Abingdon 2008). The best modern survey is E. Roesdahl, *The Vikings*, 3rd ed. (Harmondsworth 2016). Of basic books on the art of the Scandinavian world in the Viking Age, most up-to-date is J. Graham-Campbell, *Viking art* (London 2013). D. M. Wilson and O. Klindt-Jensen, *Viking Art*, (London 1966), I am told, is still useful.

For sculpture, see R. N. *Bailey, Viking Age sculpture in Northern England* (London 1980); his views are updated in his volumes in the British Academy's *Corpus of Anglo-Saxon Stone Sculpture* (Oxford 1984-). For the Scandinavian styles in the homeland and in Britain, see S. H. Fuglesang, *Some aspects of the Ringerike Style. A phase of eleventh-century art* (Odense 1980). See also D. M. Wilson, 'Jellinge-style sculpture in Northern England' in M. C. Stang and K. B. Aavitsland (eds.), *Ornament and order. Essays on Viking and Northern Medieval art for Signe Horn Fuglesang* (Trondheim 2008), 21-28. See also U. O'Meadhra, 1979/87, *Early Christian, Viking and Romanesque art. Motif-pieces from Ireland...* (Uppsala/ Stockholm 1979-87). Theses and papers in North-European archaeology 7 and 17.

An excellent popular short guide to Norse mythology is R. I. Page, *Norse myths* (London 1990). For bolder souls E. O. G. Turville-Petre, *Myth and religion of the North* (London 1964). For Sigurd, see E. Ploss, *Siegfried-Sigurd, der Drachenkämpfer. Untersuchungen zur germanischen-deutschen Heldensage* (Bonn 1966). For translations of the Sigurd story, see C. Larrington, *The Poetic Edda* (Oxford 1996), and the excellent, but now thought to be outdated, M. Schlauch, *The Saga of the Volsungs* (London 1930). For Sigurd on Norwegian stave-churches, see E. B. Hohler, *Norwegian stave church sculpture* (Oslo 1999). See also S. Margeson, 'On the iconography of the Manx crosses' in Fell (1983), 95-106; D. M. Wilson, 'Regin's smithy', *The Antiquarian: Newsletter of the Isle of Man Natural History and Antiquarian Society*, 7, 2012, 4-19. L. Kopar's wide-ranging *Gods and settlers. The iconography of Norse mythology in Anglo-Scandinavian sculpture* (Turnhout 2012), seems to be largely desk-based and excludes most of the western parallels with passing reference to the Isle of Man.

Chapter 6

The study of runes is highly specialised; readers, therefore, are here referred to a small number of books which are reasonably intelligible, but it should be noted that a text of a complete critical account of the corpus of Manx runes by M. P. Barnes and J. Knirk now awaits publication. The transliterations used in this chapter are based on their latest critical readings, which they have kindly given me. Much of the specialist literature, including the great national corpuses of runic inscriptions, is in the Scandinavian or German languages, which are referred to in the books listed here. The only study of the Manx runic inscriptions, although published in 1954, was based on those collected by Magnus Olsen in a 1911 visit; it is still useful, if needing a health warning, 'Runic inscriptions in Great Britain, Ireland and the Isle of Man', in H. Shetelig (ed.), *Viking antiquities in Great Britain and Ireland*, 6 (Oslo 1954), 151-254. For recent articles on Manx runes, see two chapters in R. I. Page, *Runes and runic inscriptions. Collected essays on Anglo-Saxon and Viking runes* (Woodbridge 1995). For transliteration, but not translation, of the inscriptions, see Page in Fell (1983), 133-46. For analysis of personal names see J. Jesch, *The Viking diaspora* (Abingdon 2015), 113-5.

The best modern general introduction to runes is M. P. Barnes, *Runes, a handbook* (Woodbridge 2012). The following works in English are indispensable: M. P. Barnes and R. Page, *The Scandinavian runic inscriptions of Britain* (Uppsala 2006), Runologiska bidrag utgivna av Institutionen for nordiska språk vid Uppsala Universitet 19; E. Moltke, *Runes and their origin. Denmark and elsewhere* (Copenhagen 1985); S. B. F. Jansson, *Runes in Sweden* (Stockholm 1987); T. Spurkland, *Norwegian runes and runic inscriptions* (Woodbridge 2005).

Appendix

A HAND-LIST OF MANX CROSSES

[1] The Kermode references provide description and figure numbers in *Manx Crosses*, 2nd ed. 1994.

[2] These measurements are for the total length of the crosses, out of the ground or their mounts.

Inv. no. Kermode *Manx Crosses* 2nd. ed.[1]	Find-place NGR SC	Present location	Maximum measure-ment[2]	Period (? = not known) Inscription	Remarks and fig. reference to this book
Inv. no. 1 Kermode 1	Rushen, Ballaqueeney 207685	Manx Museum	113cm	6th century Ogam	Fig. 3 left
Inv. no. 2 Kermode 2	Rushen, Ballaqueeney 207685	Manx Museum	52cm	6th century Ogam	
Inv. no. 3 Kermode 3	Arbory, Bymacan 249703	Manx Museum	135cm	6th century Ogam	
Inv. no. 4 Kermode 4	Arbory, Bymacan 249703	Manx Museum	44cm	6th century Ogam	
Inv. no. 5 Kermode figs. A11, A12, A13	Andreas, Knock y Doonee 404022	Manx Museum	172cm	6th century Latin and ogam	Fig. 3 right
Inv. no. 6/7 Kermode 5/6	Marown, St Patrick's Chair 316779	*In situ*	188cm 132cm	Two stones in standing composite monument	Fig. 18

Inv. no. 8 Kermode 7	Malew, Keeill Unjin 264716	Malew parish church	Length 58cm	?	
Inv. no. 9 Kermode fig. B5	Patrick, Lag ny Keeilley 217745	Manx Museum	96cm	?	
Inv. no. 10 Kermode fig. B4	Patrick, Lag ny Keeilley 217745	Manx Museum	69cm	?	
Inv. no. 11	Maughold churchyard 493917	Maughold cross-house	117cm		Trench-Jellicoe, vol. 2, 241; vol. 3.
Inv. no. 12 Kermode fig. B1	Michael, Cabbyl Pherick 307888	Kirk Michael parish church	63cm	?	
Inv. no. 13 Kermode fig. B2	Jurby, Ballachurry keeill 375982	Jurby parish church	30cm	?	
Inv. no. 14 Kermode fig. D2	German, Knocksharry 275857	Manx Museum	81cm	? pre-Scandinavian	
Inv. no. 15 Kermode fig. B3	Patrick, Lag ny Keeilley 217745	Manx Museum	101cm	? 7/9th century	
Inv. no. 16 Kermode fig. B2	Jurby, Ballachurry keeill 375982	Jurby parish church	37cm	?	
Inv. no. 17 Kermode fig. B6	Marown, Keeill Vreeshey 331801	Lost	15cm	? pre-Scandinavian	

Inv. no. 18 Kermode no. 14	Jurby, West Nappin Keeill 347981	Private ownership	43cm	? pre-Scandinavian	
Inv. no. 19 Kermode fig. C4	Patrick, Ballaquayle 257813	Manx Museum	53cm	? pre-Scandinavian	
Inv. no. 20 Kermode 12	Braddan Old Churchyard 364768	Lost	c.60cm	?	
Inv. no. 21 Kermode fig. C1	Maughold churchyard 493917	Maughold cross-house	41cm	?	
Inv. no. 22 Kermode fig. D3	Braddan, Keeill Abban 360822	St Luke's church (Keeill Abban)	46cm	?	
Inv. no. 23 Kermode no. 9	Lonan, outside churchyard 427794	Lonan cross-shelter	61cm	7/9th century	
Inv. no. 24 Kermode no. 10	Maughold churchyard 493917	Maughold cross-house	114cm	7/9th century	
Inv. no. 25 Kermode no. 11	Onchan Vicarage 400781	Onchan parish church	61cm	7/9th century	
Inv. no. 26 Kermode fig. B7	Marown, St Trinian's Chapel 317802	St Trinian's Chapel	76cm	7/9th century	
Inv. no. 27 Kermode no. 8	Lonan Old Church 427794	Lonan cross-shelter	53cm	7/9th century	

Inv. no. 28 Kermode no. 13	Malew, Kerrookeeill 260740	Malew parish church	61cm	7/9th century	
Inv. no. 29 Kermode no. 34	Santon parish church 310711	Santon parish church	114cm	6th century Latin	Fig. 4
Inv. no. 30 Kermode no. 16	German, St Patrick's Isle 242845	Manx Museum	47cm	? 8/9th century	
Inv. no. 31 Kermode no. 15	German, St Patrick's Isle 242845	Manx Museum	38cm	? 8/9th century	
Inv. no. 32 Kermode no. 17	Maughold parish church 4939174	Maughold cross-house	35cm	8/9th century	
Inv. no. 33 Kermode no. 18	Maughold Keeill Woirrey 433894	Maughold cross-house	99cm	8/9th century	
Inv. no. 34 Kermode fig. B10	Patrick, Lag ny Keeilley 217745	Manx Museum	80cm	8/9th century	
Inv. no. 35 Kermode no. 19	German, St Patrick's Isle 242845	Manx Museum	159cm	8/9th century	
Inv. no. 36 Kermode fig. C2	Andreas parish church 415992	Andreas parish church	51cm	?	
Inv. no. 37 Kermode fig. B14	Andreas, Knock y Doonee 404022	Andreas parish church	20cm	8/9th century	

Inv. no. 38 Kermode fig. B13	German, Banff Place 300813	Manx Museum	81cm	?	
Inv. no. 39 Kermode no. 20	Maughold parish church 493917	Maughold cross- house	58cm	8/9th century	
Inv. no. 40 Kermode fig. C3	Maughold, Keeill Woirrey 433894	Maughold cross- house	106cm	8/9th century	
Inv. no. 41 Kermode no. 21	Maughold churchyard 493917	Maughold cross- house	55cm	8/9th century Greek *omega*	Fig. 11
Inv. no. 42 Kermode no. 25	Maughold churchyard 493917	Maughold cross- house	111cm	8/9th century A.S. runes	Fig. 16
Inv. no. 43 Kermode no. 117	Maughold churchyard 493917	Maughold cross- house	55cm	8/9th century A.S. runes	
Inv. no. 44 Kermode fig. B8	Marown, Ballaquinney 333777	St Trinian's Chapel	35cm	7/8th century	
Inv. no. 45 Kermode fig. B9	Marown, Ballaquinney 333777	Lost	28cm	?	
Inv. no. 46 Kermode no. 26	Maughold, Ballakilley 492917	Maughold cross- house	61cm	7/8th century	
Inv. no. 47 Kermode no. 27	Maughold churchyard 493917	Maughold cross- house	68cm	7/8th century Latin	Fig. 13

Inv. no. 48 Kermode no. 28	Maughold churchyard 493917	Maughold cross-house	145cm	7/8th century	
Inv. no. 49 Kermode no. 24	Patrick, Ballelby Keeill 220788	Private owner	220cm	?	
Inv. no. 50 Kermode no. 22	Marown Old Parish Church 321786	Old Parish Church (St Runius)	160cm	8/9th century	
Inv. no. 51 Kermode no. 23	Maughold churchyard 493917	Maughold cross-house	38cm	8/9th century	Fig. 17
Inv. no. 52 Kermode fig. B16	Bride, Ballavarkish 460007	Bride parish church	58cm	8/9th century Ogam and Latin	Fig. 12
Inv. no. 53 Kermode no. 29	Maughold churchyard 493917	Maughold cross-house	122cm	? 9th century	
Inv. no. 54 Kermode no. 30	Maughold churchyard 493917	Maughold cross-house	35cm	? 9th century	
Inv. no. 55 Kermode no. 31	Maughold 'Clerk's Glebe' 493917	Maughold cross-house	96cm	9th century	
Inv. no. 56 Kermode no. 32	Maughold, Cooil Ard 452873	Maughold cross-house	84cm	9th century	
Inv. no. 57 Kermode no. 33	Maughold, Ballaglass 461904	Maughold cross-house	76cm	9th century	

Inv. no. 58 Kermode no. 44	Bride, ?churchyard 449012	Bride parish church	121cm, now 66cm	? pre-Scandinavian	
Inv. no. 59 Kermode no. 45	Maughold churchyard 493917	Maughold cross-house	144cm	9th century	
Inv. no. 60 Kermode fig. B12	Andreas churchyard 415992	Andreas parish church	38cm	9th century	
Inv. no. 61 Kermode no. 50	Rushen, Calf of Man 1666	Manx Museum	66cm	10th century	Fig. 51
Inv. no. 62 Kermode no. 35	Santon, Sulbrick Keeill 309746	Santon parish church	137cm	9th century	See also *Manx. Mus. Journal*, iv: 61, p.163ff, pl.175, 7
Inv. no. 63 Kermode no. 36	Braddan Old Churchyard 364768	Braddan Old Church	91cm	9th century	
Inv. no. 64 Kermode no. 37	Braddan Old Churchyard 364768	Braddan Old Church	88cm	9th century	
Inv. no. 65 Kermode fig. C5	Braddan, Middle Farm 358746	Braddan Old Church	167cm	9th century	
Inv. no. 66 Kermode no. 47	Rushen, Ballaglonney 200703	Manx Museum	96cm	? 8/9th century	Fig. 23
Inv. no. 67 Kermode no. 46	German, St Patrick's Isle 241845	Manx Museum	46cm	8/9th century	

Inv. no. 68 Kermode no. 38	Maughold churchyard 493917	Maughold cross-house	132cm	9th century	Fig. 20
Inv. no. 69 Kermode no. 48	Maughold, Port y Vullen 476926	Maughold cross-house	213cm	9th century Latin uncial	Figs. 9 and 10
Inv. no. 70 Kermode no. 39	Maughold churchyard 493917	Maughold cross-house	157cm	9th century	
Inv. no. 71 Kermode no. 49	Lonan, Ballalheaney, Glen Roy 405839	Lonan cross-shelter	188cm	9th century	Fig. 22
Inv. no. 72 Kermode no. 69	Braddan Old Churchyard 364768	Braddan Old Church	132cm	9/10th century	Fig. 25 right
Inv. no. 73 Kermode no. 57	Lonan Old Churchyard 427794	Lonan Old Church-yard	c.251cm	9/10th century	Fig. 25 left Fig. 28
Inv. no. 74 Kermode no. 61	Onchan churchyard 400781	Onchan parish church	66cm	9/10th century	
Inv. no. 75 Kermode no. 40	Lonan Old Churchyard 427794	Lonan cross-shelter	55cm	9th century	
Inv. no. 76 Kermode no. 42	Lonan Old Churchyard 427794	Lonan cross-shelter	152cm	9/10th century	
Inv. no. 77 Kermode no. 41	Lonan Old Churchyard 427794	Lonan cross-shelter	46cm	9/10th century	

Inv. no. 78 Kermode no. 56	Braddan Old Churchyard 364768	Braddan Old Church	183cm	9/10th century	
Inv. no. 79 Kermode no. 51	Maughold, Keeill Chiggyrt 483898	Maughold cross-house	86cm	Early 10th century	Fig. 54
Inv. no. 80 Kermode no. 65	Maughold parish church 493917	Maughold cross-house	206cm	? 10th century	
Inv. no. 81 Kermode no. 43	Marown Old Church 321786	Marown Old Church	158cm	? 10th century	
Inv. no. 82 Kermode no. 52	Maughold Vicarage 492917	Maughold cross-house	60cm	? early 10th century	
Inv. no. 83 Kermode no. 53	Lezayre churchyard 423941	Lezayre parish church	53cm	9/10th century	
Inv. no. 84 Kermode no. 58	Maughold churchyard 493917	Maughold cross-house	56cm	Early 10th century	
Inv. no. 85 Kermode no. 59	Onchan churchyard 400781	Onchan parish church	149cm	10th century	Fig. 24
Inv. no. 86 Kermode no. 60	Maughold, Cardle Veg 455901	Maughold cross-house	25cm	? 9/10th century	
Inv. no. 87 Kermode fig. C8	Maughold 'Clerk's House' 492917	Maughold cross-house	28cm	9/10th century	

Inv. no. 88 Kermode no. 70	Maughold parish church 493917	Maughold cross-house	25cm	? 9th century	Part of no. 89
Inv. no. 89 Kermode no. 71	Maughold parish church 493917	Maughold cross-house	19cm	? 9th century	Part of no. 88
Inv. no. 90 Kermode no. 54	Maughold churchyard 493917	Maughold cross-house	162cm	9th century	
Inv. no. 91 Kermode no. 55	Maughold churchyard 493917	Maughold cross-house	231cm	9th century	
Inv. no. 92 Kermode no. 62	Onchan churchyard 400781	Onchan parish church	135cm	9th century	Fig. 27
Inv. no. 93 Kermode no. 63	Onchan ?churchyard 400781	Onchan parish church	127cm	9th century	
Inv. no. 94 Kermode no. 64	Michael, Bishopscourt 328924	Kirk Michael parish church	190cm	9/10th century	
Inv. no. 95 Kermode no. 68	Santon, Balnahowe 333719	Santon parish church	52cm	8/9th century	
Inv. no. 96 Kermode no. 67	Maughold churchyard 493917	Maughold cross-house	142cm	9th century	Fig. 21
Inv. no. 97 Kermode no. 66	Maughold church 493917	Maughold cross-house	162cm	9/10th century	Fig. 29

Inv. no. 98 Kermode no. 72	Maughold Green 492917	Maughold cross-house	277cm		
Inv. no. 99 Kermode no. 73	Andreas Green 415993	Andreas parish church	246cm	9/10th century Scand. runes	
Inv. no. 100 Kermode no. 76	Rushen, Ballaqueeney 206686	Four Roads, Port St Mary	335cm	10th century Scandinavian	
Inv. no. 101 Kermode no. 74	Michael Old Church 318908	Kirk Michael parish church	183cm	10th century Scand. runes	Fig. 32
Inv. no. 102 Kermode no. 75	Michael churchyard 317908	Kirk Michael parish church	129cm	10th century Scand. runes	
Inv. no. 103 Kermode no. 78	Jurby, West Nappin 347981	Jurby parish church	208cm	10th century Scandinavian	
Inv. no. 104 Kermode no. 79	Jurby churchyard 349985	Jurby parish church	56cm	9/10th century	
Inv. no. 105 Kermode no. 80	Jurby churchyard 349985	Jurby parish church	17cm	?	
Inv. no. 106 Kermode no. 77	Ballaugh Old Church 341957	Ballaugh Old Church	137cm	10th century Scand. runes	Fig. 33
Inv. no. 107 Kermode no. 81	German, St John's Chapel 279818	St John's Chapel	135cm	10th century Scand. runes	

Inv. no. 108 Kermode no. 82	Maughold parish church 493917	Maughold cross-house	114cm	10th century Scandinavian	
Inv. no. 109 Kermode no. 83	Andreas Rectory 414994	Andreas parish church	61cm	10th century Scandinavian	
Inv. no. 110 Kermode no. 85	Michael churchyard 317908	Kirk Michael parish church	89cm	10th century Scand. runes	
Inv. no. 111 Kermode no. 84	Andreas churchyard 415992	Andreas parish church	56cm	10th century Scand. runes	Fig. 58
Inv. no. 112 Kermode no. 86	Braddan Old Churchyard 364768	Old Kirk Braddan	152cm	10th century Scand. runes	
Inv. no. 113 Kermode no. 87	Andreas Rectory 414994	Andreas parish church	86cm	10th century Scand. runes	
Inv. no. 114 Kermode no. 91	Maughold parish church 493917	Maughold cross-house	53cm	10th century Scandinavian	Fig. 31
Inv. no. 115 Kermode no. 88	German, St Patrick's Isle 241845	Manx Museum	46cm	10th century Scandinavian	
Inv. no. 116 Kermode no. 90	Michael churchyard 317908	Kirk Michael parish church	39cm	10/11th century Scandinavian	Fig. 40
Inv. no. 117 Kermode no. 89	Michael Old Churchyard 318908	Kirk Michael parish church	138cm	?10th century	Fig. 39

Inv. no. 118 Kermode no. 92	Bride Old Church 449012	Bride parish church	112cm	10th century Scand. runes	
Inv. no. 119 Kermode no. 93	Jurby Ballaconley Keeill 383000	Jurby parish church	213cm	10th century Scandinavian	Fig. 43
Inv. no. 120 Kermode no. 94	Malew churchyard 268694	Malew parish church	152cm	10th century Scandinavian	Fig. 36
Inv. no. 121 Kermode no. 95	Andreas churchyard 415992	Andreas parish church	68cm	10th century Scandinavian	Fig. 42
Inv. no. 122 Kermode no. 96	Maughold, Ramsey 455941	Maughold cross-house	117cm	10/11th century Scandinavian	Figs. 41 and 45
Inv. no. 123 Kermode fig. B17	Michael, outside churchyard 318908	Kirk Michael parish church	41cm	10th century Scand. runes	Fig. 56
Inv. no. 124 Kermode no. 97	Bride parish church 449012	Bride parish church	142cm	10th century	
Inv. no. 125 Kermode no. 98	Jurby churchyard 349985	Jurby parish church	79cm	10th century Scandinavian	Fig. 44
Inv. no. 126 Kermode no. 100	Michael Old Church 318908	Kirk Michael parish church	98cm	10th century Scand. runes	Fig. 35
Inv. no. 127 Kermode no. 99	Jurby churchyard 349985	Jurby parish church	76cm	10th century Scand. runes	Fig. 50

Inv. no. 128 Kermode no. 102	Andreas ?churchyard 415992	Andreas parish church	35cm	10th century Scandinavian	Fig. 49
Inv. no. 129 Kermode no. 101	Michael churchyard 317908	Kirk Michael parish church	47cm	10th century Scand. runes	Fig. 52
Inv. no. 130 Kermode no. 104	Michael churchyard 317908	Kirk Michael parish church	176cm	10th cent. Scand. runes and ogam	
Inv. no. 131 Kermode no. 103	Andreas churchyard 415992	Andreas parish church	193cm	10th century Scand. runes	Fig. 30
Inv. no. 132 Kermode no. 105	Michael churchyard 317908	Kirk Michael parish church	235cm	10th century Scandinavian	Fig. 55
Inv. no. 133 Kermode no. 106	Maughold, Ballagilley Keeill 459916	Maughold cross-house	20cm	10th century Scand. runes	
Inv. no. 134 Kermode no. 107	Jurby churchyard 349985	Jurby parish church	66cm	10th century Scandinavian	
Inv. no. 135 Kermode no. 108	Braddan Old Churchyard 364768	Old Kirk Braddan	213cm	Late 10th century Scand. runes	Fig. 37
Inv. no. 136 Kermode no. 109	Braddan, Old Kirk Braddan 364768	Old Kirk Braddan	122cm	Late 10th century Scand. runes	Fig. 38
Inv. no. 137	Braddan, Old Kirk Braddan 364768	Lost			

Inv. no. 138 Kermode no. 110	Braddan ?Old Churchyard 364768	Old Kirk Braddan	39cm	10th century Scand. runes	Fig. 60
Inv. no. 139 Kermode no. 111	Marown, Rheynn Farm 350808	St Trinian's Chapel	53cm	10th century Scand. runes	
Inv. no. 140 Kermode no. 112	German, north transept of cathedral 242845	Manx Museum	68cm	10th century Scand. runes	
Inv. no. 141 Kermode no. 113	Onchan, a garden 397782	Onchan parish church	114cm	10th century Scand. runes	Fig. 61
Inv. no. 142 Kermode fig. C9	Maughold churchyard 493917	Maughold cross-house	76cm	11th century Scandinavian	Fig. 57
Inv. no. 143 Kermode no. D4	Jurby, Ballaconley Keeill 383000	Jurby parish church	30cm		
Inv. no. 144 Kermode no. 114	Maughold, Keeill Woirrey 433894	Maughold cross-house	69cm	12th century runes and ogam	
Inv. no. 145 Kermode no. 115	Maughold parish church 493917	Maughold cross-house	33cm	12th century	Fig. 62
Inv. no. 146 Kermode fig. D5	Braddan Old Churchyard 364768	Old Kirk Braddan	36cm	9/10th century	
Inv. no. 147 Bride		Later architectural feature			

Inv. no. 148 Kermode fig. E1	German, Keeill Moirrey 261834	Manx Museum	91cm	?	
Inv. no. 149 Kermode fig. E6	Maughold churchyard 493917	Maughold cross-house	24cm	9th century	
Inv. no. 150 Kermode fig. E5:1	Lezayre, Cronk yn How 436956	Lezayre parish church	67cm	?	
Inv. no. 151 Kermode fig. E3:2	Lezayre, Cronk yn How 436956	Lezayre parish church	41cm	?	
Inv. no. 152 Kermode fig. E4:1	Lezayre, Cronk yn How 436956	Lezayre parish church	51cm	?	
Inv. no. 153 Kermode fig. E4:3	Lezayre, Cronk yn How 436956	Lezayre parish church	50cm	?	
Inv. no. 154 Kermode fig. E4:2	Lezayre, Cronk yn Howe 436956	Lezayre parish church	62cm	?	
Inv. no. 155 Kermode fig. E5:2	Lezayre, Cronk yn Howe 436956	Lezayre parish church	62cm	?	
Inv. no. 156 Kermode fig. E3:3	Lezayre, Cronk yn Howe 436956	Lezayre parish church	26cm	?	
Inv. no. 157 Kermode fig. E4:5	Lezayre, Cronk yn Howe 436956	Lezayre parish church	39cm	?	

Inv. no. 158 Kermode fig. E3:1	Lezayre, Cronk yn How 436956	Lezayre parish church	55cm	?	Multiple graffiti present
Inv. no. 159 Kermode fig. E4:4	Lezayre, Cronk yn How 436956	Lezayre parish church	23cm	?	
Inv. no. 160	Lonan, ?Ballamiljyn Keeill 427844	Lonan cross-shelter	Length 25cm		
Inv. no. 161 Kermode fig. E2	Maughold, Port y Vullen 472929	Manx Museum	Length 9.5cm		
Inv. no. 162	Patrick, Keeill Cragh 245821	Manx Museum	14cm		
Inv. no. 163	Maughold, Keeill Chiggyrt 483898	Maughold cross-house	83cm		
Inv. no. 164	Malew, Ronaldsway 290686	Manx Museum	Length 66cm	7/8th century	Fig. 15
Inv. no. 165	Malew, Ronaldsway 289682	Manx Museum	53cm		*Antiquaries Journal*, 20:1, 1940, 76-7
Inv. no. 166	Malew, Ronaldsway 290686	Manx Museum	76cm		Ibid, *loc. cit.*

Inv. no. 167	Lezayre, Ballamanagh 391939	Manx Museum	63cm		*Journal Mx. Mus.* IV:61. Pl.172, 3
Inv. no. 168	Andreas churchyard 415992	Andreas parish church	91cm	?	Ibid. Pl.172, 4
Inv. no. 169	Maughold churchyard 493917	Manx Museum	56cm	8/9th cent. Latin uncial	Fig. 8
Inv. no. 170	German, Banff Place 300813	Manx Museum	51cm	?	*Journal Mx. Mus.*VII:82. Pl. 8
Inv. no. 171	Braddan, Speke Keill 333746	Manx Museum	126cm	?	Ibid, *loc. cit.*
Inv. no. 172	Maughold village 492917	Maughold cross-house	121cm	?	Ibid, *loc. cit.*
Inv. no. 173	Lezayre, Cronk yn How 436956	Manx Museum	74cm	?	
Inv. no. 174	Patrick, Lag ny Keeilley 217745	Manx Museum	45cm	?	*Journal Mx. Mus.*VII:82. Pl. 8
Inv. no. 175	Maughold village 492917	Manx Museum	97cm	10/11th cent. Scand. runes	Ibid, Pl.7
Inv. no. 176	Braddan Old Churchyard 364768	Old Kirk Braddan	25cm	10/11th cent. Scand. runes	Ibid, *loc. cit.*
Inv. no. 177	Lonan, Barroose 423814	Manx Museum	48cm	?	Ibid, Pl.8
Inv. no. 178	Michael Churchyard 317908	Manx Museum	15cm	?	

Inv. no. 179	Jurby churchyard 349985	Jurby parish church	28cm	?	
Inv. no. 180	Rushen, Croit y Caley 223692	Manx Museum	72cm	?	
Inv. no. 181	Patrick, Lag ny Keeilley 217745	Manx Museum	64cm	?	
Inv. no. 182	German, Cronk Breck Keeill 296814	Manx Museum	41cm	7/8th century	Decorated pebble, *Journal Mx. Mus.*VII:88. Pl.52
Inv. no. 183	Michael, Keeill Vael 371888	Manx Museum	29cm	?	Morris, 1983, 127-8
Inv. no. 184	Michael, Keeill Vael 371888	Manx Museum	53cm	?	Ibid., *loc.cit.*
Inv. no. 185	Michael, Keeill Vael 371888	Manx Museum	43cm	?	Ibid., *loc.cit.*
Inv. no. 186	Michael, Keeill Vael 371888	Manx Museum	68cm	?	Ibid., *loc.cit.*
Inv. no. 187	Michael, Keeill Vael 371888	Manx Museum	17cm	?	Ibid., *loc.cit.*
Inv. no. 188	Michael, Keeill Vael 371888	Manx Museum	64cm	?	Ibid., *loc.cit.*
Inv. no. 189	Braddan, Speke Keeill 333746	Manx Museum	94cm	?	
Inv. no. 190	Maughold churchyard 493917	Maughold cross-house	69cm	?8th century	

Inv. no. 191	German, St Patrick's Isle 242845	Manx Museum	30cm	?9/10th century	Freke 2002, 287-8. Fig. 88:3
Inv. no. 192	German, St Patrick's Isle 242845	Manx Museum	24cm	Post-11th century	Ibid. Fig. 88:4
Inv. no. 193	Andreas, Larivane Croft 411998	Manx Museum	17cm	10th century	*TIMNHAS*, 9:4, 601-5
Inv. no. 194	Michael, Bishopscourt 328924	Manx Museum	105cm	9/10th century	Trench-Jellicoe 1999[3]
Inv. no. 195	German, St Patrick's Isle 242845	Manx Museum	8.3cm	8/9th century	?trial-piece Freke 2002, 288-9. Fig. 88:1
Inv. no. 196	German, St Patrick's Isle 241845	Manx Museum	16cm	?10/11th century	Graffito Ibid, 289. Fig. 88:2
Inv. no. 197	German, St Patrick's Isle 242845	Manx Museum	31.5cm	?10/11th century	Ibid., 290. Fig. 89:5
Inv. no. 198	German, St Patrick's Isle 242845	Manx Museum	42cm	7/11th century	Ibid., 289-90. Fig. 89:6
Inv. no. 199	Santon parish church 310711	Santon parish church	90cm	?	

[3] Trench-Jellicoe, 'Messages on a monument: recent recovered iconography on a Late Manx fragment from Bishopscourt', in P. J. Davey (ed.), *Recent archaeological research on the Isle of Man*, Oxford 1999, 183-7. BAR British Series 278.

Inv. no. 200	Braddan Old Church 364768	Manx Museum	34cm	10th century	
Inv. no. 201	Patrick, Lag ny Keeilley 217745	Manx Museum	33cm	?	
Inv. no. 202	Patrick, Lag ny Keeilley 217745	Manx Museum	46cm	?	
Inv. no. 203	Patrick, Lag ny Keeilley 217745	Manx Museum	67cm	?	
Inv. no. 204	German, Banff Place 300813	Manx Museum	154cm	?	*TIMNHAS*, 10.3 (1995), 289-92. Fig. 1.
Inv. no. 205	Braddan, Speke Keeill 333746	Manx Museum	33cm	Scholastic ogam	

INDEX